TOURO COLLEGE LIBRARY
Kings Hwy

WITHDRAWN

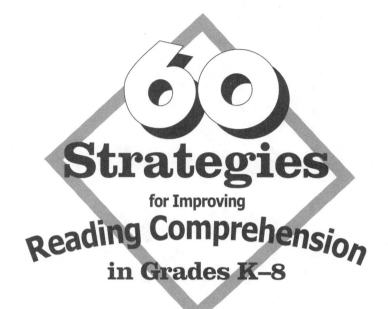

60 Strategies

for Improving

Reading Comprehension

in Grades K–8

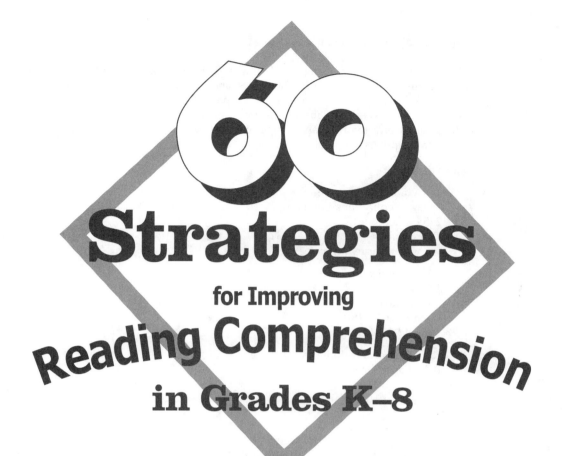

60 Strategies

for Improving
Reading Comprehension
in Grades K–8

TOURO COLLEGE LIBRARY
Kings Hwy

Kathleen Feeney Jonson

CORWIN PRESS
A SAGE Publications Company
Thousand Oaks, California

KH

Copyright © 2006 by Corwin Press

All rights reserved. When forms and sample documents are included, their use is authorized only by educators, local school sites, and/or noncommercial entities who have purchased the book. Except for that usage, no part of this book may be reproduced or utilized in any form or by any means, electronic or mechanical, including photocopying, recording, or by any information storage and retrieval system, without permission in writing from the publisher.

For information:

Corwin Press
A Sage Publications Company
2455 Teller Road
Thousand Oaks, California 91320
www.corwinpress.com

SAGE Publications Ltd
1 Oliver's Yard
55 City Road
London EC1Y 1SP
United Kingdom

Sage Publications India Pvt. Ltd.
B-42, Panchsheel Enclave
Post Box 4109
New Delhi 110 017 India

Printed in the United States of America

Library of Congress Cataloging-in-Publication Data

Jonson, Kathleen Feeney.
60 strategies for improving reading comprehension in grades K-8 /
by Kathleen Feeney Jonson.
   p. cm.
Includes bibliographical references and index.
ISBN 0-7619-8837-8 (cloth) – ISBN 0-7619-8838-6 (pbk.)
   1. Reading comprehension—Study and teaching (Elementary)
2. Reading—Aids and devices. I. Title: Sixty strategies for improving reading comprehension in grades K-8. II. Title.
LB1573.7.J66 2006
428.4'071—dc22   2005021146

This book is printed on acid-free paper.

05   06   07   08   09   10   9   8   7   6   5   4   3   2   1

Acquisitions Editor:	Rachel Livsey
Editorial Assistant:	Phyllis Cappello
Production Editor:	Kristen Gibson
Copy Editor:	Teresa Berensfeld
Typesetter:	C&M Digitals (P) Ltd.
Indexer:	Kay Dusheck
Proofreader:	Maria L. Alonzo
Cover Designer:	Lisa Miller

8/11/06

Contents

Preface

One of the main goals of teachers of reading is to help students learn to comprehend text. In these days post-NRP (National Reading Panel Report 2000), most of us are well aware of the importance of teaching readers to be strategic. We have learned that good readers apply a variety of processes to make sense out of print. We know that students who succeed in comprehending text are actively involved in the reading processes—processes that require the ability to make predictions, to confirm or disaffirm those predictions, to ask questions, to infer and visualize, and to monitor understanding as they read. We know that skilled readers have schemata for particular topics, text structures, metacognitive activities, and forms of language, and they draw on those schemata as they read. These readers use prior knowledge interactively with new information in the text. They apply a variety of strategies simultaneously to facilitate comprehension. Reading comprehension is clearly not the mastery of isolated skills or the verbatim reproduction of information as it appears on the page.

Many of us constantly look for new ways to help our students with such important comprehension processes as predicting, visualizing, making inferences, monitoring, synthesizing, and summarizing. Through studying professional texts and attending staff development sessions, teachers familiarize themselves with strategies and materials to teach these processes to students across the grades. Most of us have favorites—strategies we like to teach and strategies we know work well for our students. But we are always looking for more good ideas. The purpose of this book is to add to the teacher's repertoire of strategies and perhaps to provide a new focus on tried and true favorites.

Volumes of research have attempted to identify which strategies skilled readers use most often. When we examine these studies as a whole, we find a group of *meta-strategies* that emerge as being key for understanding as we read. Although the research literature discusses many other strategies, these seven appear to have the greatest support. Today these meta-strategies have a major impact on how reading comprehension is being taught in the United States:

- *Making connections* (finding ties within the text, to another text, from known information to new information, to your life, to the world)
- *Monitoring reading for meaning* (sometimes called *clarifying*; knowing what's not making sense and applying "fix-up" strategies as necessary)

- *Determining important information* (identifying the story line in narrative texts and main ideas in expository texts; distinguishing main ideas from details)
- *Visualizing* (creating images in your mind; "seeing the story" in your mind's eye)
- *Asking questions* (generating questions from the text, the author, yourself)
- *Making inferences* (predicting, wondering, assessing what is going on)
- *Summarizing and synthesizing* (applying new knowledge to what is known and generating new ideas)

In the National Reading Panel Report, comprehension strategies are defined as "specific procedures that guide students to become aware of how well they are comprehending as they attempt to read" (NRP, pp. 4–40). For example, students may be taught to generate questions about the text as they read—usually of the *why, what, how, when,* or *where* variety. By generating and trying to answer these questions, the reader processes the text more actively (NRP, pp. 4–40). The value of the cognitive meta-strategies for comprehension instruction is that they provide a way for teachers to break through students' passivity and involve them in their own learning. Another important value of cognitive strategies in comprehension instruction is their "usefulness in the development of instructional procedures" (NRP, pp. 4–40).

The value of a book like this one is just what the NRP describes: It provides teachers with a toolkit of learning strategies that are designed to actively engage students in comprehension processes and that were developed as specific instructional procedures with clearly delineated steps for implementation. The strategies are arranged alphabetically for easy reference. Grade-level recommendations for the use of each instructional strategy are offered. Goals for each strategy are outlined under the heading "Why Do We Use It?" with reference to many of the big seven metacognitive meta-strategies. Directions on how to implement the instructional strategy are provided in a similar clear, coherent format throughout the book. Graphics and examples are provided to illustrate the strategies. Finally, the book includes references and additional information to help teachers modify and expand the use of the strategies in their own classrooms.

This text is a reflection of my ongoing efforts to assist preservice and inservice teachers in their efforts to teach students effectively in the busy world of real-life schools. Many people have provided input and support in the development of this book. I am indebted to the children, teachers, and administrators I have worked with in Seattle and San Francisco communities over the last thirty-five years. They have helped me to understand and refine my beliefs about effective reading instruction. In particular, I want to thank the graduate students in my reading courses at the University of San Francisco. Their questions and insights constantly press me into lifelong learning and reflection. Many of them generously shared ideas and materials for this book, and I am most grateful to them: Stephanie Abramowitz, Caryn Barry, China Byon, Stephanie Chin, Jenn Jurcy, Lindsay Kahn, Christine Labagh, Eliza Lurie, Brooke Nylen,

Amanda Rawls, Kristina Reguero, Brooke Sibley, Julie Song, Tobi Slavet, Matt Sullivan, Julie Walton, Kate Working, and many others. College professors and literacy professionals from across the country also reviewed the draft manuscript and provided valuable suggestions for improvements. In particular, the contributions of the following reviewers are gratefully acknowledged:

Nancy L. Witherell, EdD
Professor, Chair, Department of Elementary and Early Childhood
   Education
Bridgewater State College
Bridgewater, MA

Sandra Anderson
Consultant
Exemplary Education LLC
Newcastle, WA

Dr. Paul G. Young
Executive Director (Retired Principal)
West After School Center
(formerly West Elementary School)
Lancaster, OH

Terry Matherne
Director of Literacy
St. Charles Parish Public Schools
Luling, LA

Dr. Scott Mandel
Teacher
Los Angeles Unified School District
Los Angeles, CA

Mary C. McMackin
Professor
Lesley University
Cambridge, MA

Sharon Toomey Clark, PhD
Teacher
Montera Elementary School
Ontario-Montclair School District
Montclair, CA

Mitzi Chizek
Principal
Dallas Center-Grimes High School
Grimes, IA

Finally, I am indebted to Barbara Fuller of editcetera in Berkeley, California, who gave me invaluable assistance with this project, and to Maurie Manning, whose sprightly illustrations enliven the book. I am also thankful for the advice and patience of Rachel Livsey, acquisitions editor at Corwin Press. With this book, I am honored to be a Corwin author for the third time. To all of the individuals who made it possible, I say a heart-felt "Thank you."

● REFERENCE

National Reading Panel. (2000). *Teaching children to read: An evidence-based assessment of the scientific research literature on reading and its implications for reading instruction.* Washington, DC: National Institute of Child Health and Human Development.

About the Author

Kathleen Feeney Jonson, EdD, in her thirty-five years as an educator has taught at the elementary and secondary levels, served as a reading specialist, director of staff development, principal, director of curriculum and instruction, and university faculty member. She has conducted numerous workshops for teachers and administrators on such topics as reading comprehension strategies, writing process, portfolio assessment, peer coaching, and beginning teacher assistance programs. Dr. Jonson is currently professor and coordinator of the Master in Arts in Teaching Reading program in the School of Education of the University of San Francisco. This is her third book with Corwin Press. Other titles include *The New Elementary Teacher's Handbook, 2nd edition* (2001), and *Being an Effective Mentor: How to Help Beginning Teachers Succeed* (2002).

**CORWIN
PRESS**

The Corwin Press logo—a raven striding across an open book—represents the union of courage and learning. Corwin Press is committed to improving education for all learners by publishing books and other professional development resources for those serving the field of PreK–12 education. By providing practical, hands-on materials, Corwin Press continues to carry out the promise of its motto: **"Helping Educators Do Their Work Better."**

ABC Book

Suggested Grade Levels: K to 8

Elements Addressed: Plot/theme, expository text

Meta-Strategies Incorporated: Determining important information, summarizing and synthesizing

Supplies: Narrative or expository text, butcher paper or flipchart, drawing paper, pens or pencils, markers or colored pencils

WHAT IS AN ABC BOOK?

An ABC book—or an alphabet book—is a student-created book with one page for each letter of the alphabet. The book is designed to incorporate important ideas from a theme or literature unit being studied in class.

When Do We Use It?

Students create an alphabet book after completing a piece of literature or a unit of study.

Why Do We Use It?

While creating these books, students review topics and content areas. They focus on important information.

How Do We Use ABC Books?

The teacher begins this strategy by showing sample books created by the teacher or former students. The teacher may also present alphabet trade books to show how they sometimes focus on themes. Next, the theme to be used as the focus for the class book is discussed.

On butcher paper or a flipchart, the teacher presents a large grid with twenty-six spaces, each labeled with one letter of the alphabet. As a class, students brainstorm to come up with theme-related words and ideas to list under each letter of the alphabet.

Each student is assigned one letter of the alphabet and asked to create a page for that letter. A sample page is shown, indicating placement of the letter, text, and illustration. The student may choose any word from the class list or come up with another word related to the theme or unit of study. Young students may write simply, "A is for ____." More advanced students may write a few sentences or a full paragraph. Students should have time to edit their work and revise it. They then illustrate the page. After all pages have been completed, the teacher binds them into a book.

Alternatively, students may be divided into small groups of, say, four students each. In this group, each student would be responsible for creating six or seven alphabet pages.

How Else Can We Use This Strategy?

Alphabet Poetry: Students may create a two-line rhyme for the letter or letters they represent.

Individual Project: Older students could create their own books. Such a project would be time-consuming, however, and would be a significant assignment requiring several days (or weeks) of work.

Where Can We Learn More?

Curtis, M. E., & Longo, A. M. (2001). Teaching vocabulary to adolescents to improve comprehension. *Reading Online.* Retrieved February 8, 2004, from http://www.readingonline.org/articles/art_index.asp?HREF=curtis/index.html

Fink, L. S. (2004). *Writing ABC books to enhance reading comprehension.* Retrieved March 3, 2005, from http://www.readwritethink.org/lessons

Guzzetti, B. J., & Wooten, C. M. (2002). Children creating artists' books: Integrating visual arts and language arts. *Reading Online.* Retrieved February 8, 2004, from http://www.readingonline.org/newliteracies/lit_index.asp?HREF=guzzetti2/index.html

Henry, L. (2004). *ABC bookmaking builds vocabulary in the content areas.* Retrieved March 3, 2005, from http://www.readwritethink.org/lessons

Spann, M. (1999). *Twenty-six interactive alphabet mini-books.* New York: Scholastic.

Tompkins, G. E. (1994). *Teaching writing: Balancing process and product* (2nd ed.). Upper Saddle River, NJ: Merrill/Prentice Hall.

Figure 1.1

Book used: Paterson, K. (1977). *Bridge to Terabithia*. New York: HarperCollins Children's Books.

Contributed by Caryn Barry, San Francisco, CA, Summer 2004.

2

Anticipation Guide

Suggested Grade Levels: 3 to 8

Elements Addressed: Plot/theme, expository text

Meta-Strategies Incorporated: Making connections, asking questions

Supplies: Narrative or expository text, handout with statements listed on it, pens or pencils

● WHAT IS AN ANTICIPATION GUIDE?

An anticipation guide is a list of teacher-created statements that students agree with or disagree with. It forces students to think about issues presented in a text.

When Do We Use It?

This strategy begins before students read. The group reevaluates after reading.

Why Do We Use It?

Anticipation guides stimulate interest in a topic and activate students' knowledge about a subject before they begin to read. The guide also helps set a purpose for reading: Because students have already been introduced to the subject matter and expressed an opinion about it, they take more interest in their reading. For example, a statement such as "Kids shouldn't have to go to school" might generate lively discussion and motivate students to read the text.

How Do We Use Anticipation Guides?

Before students begin a reading assignment, the teacher reviews the text, notes major ideas related to the assignment, and develops a list of five to ten general statements (not questions) based on those key ideas. Some of the statements are true; others are false. In choosing statements, the teacher considers what students might already know about a topic and any misconceptions they might have. The statements are designed to bring out different opinions and thus evoke discussion and debate. They may relate to the story's plot, to its theme, or to expository content. Statements should be sequenced to follow the text.

Statements are listed on a sheet of paper, copied, and handed out to all students. The teacher reads the first statement aloud and instructs students to write in the margin next to the statement "agree" or "disagree." The teacher may continue reading statements aloud, leaving time for students to respond after each, or may instruct students to work independently, noting in the margin whether they agree or disagree with each statement.

After students have completed all of their responses, the class discusses the statements as a group. Students share their responses (agree or disagree), defending their positions as they speak. They have time to respond to the views of other students. The teacher facilitates this discussion, asking follow-up questions as necessary or keeping quiet as students respond to each other.

Next, the students read the text. After they finish, they compare their original responses to what they have learned from the text. They use the text to support or refute each statement.

Figure 2.1

Anticipation Guide for
Sadako and the Thousand Paper Cranes

Please mark "agree" or "disagree" next to each of the following statements.

1. _____ When an atomic bomb is dropped during a war, no one is responsible for what happens to its victims.

2. _____ Atomic bombs should be used to end all wars.

3. _____ A person must be famous to be considered a hero or heroine.

4. _____ The United States should take responsibility for the Japanese victims of the atomic bomb.

5. _____ After a war is over, there is no winner or loser, only victims of destruction.

6. _____ When a bomb is dropped, to die instantly is better than to be injured and survive.

7. _____ Believing you can survive a terminal illness can actually help you fight the illness.

8. _____ Dying is worse for children than for adults.

9. _____ Watching someone you love die is worse than dying yourself.

10. _____ To appreciate peace, a person must first experience war.

Book used: Coerr, E. (1977). *Sadako and the thousand paper cranes.* New York: Penguin Putnam Books for Young Readers.

Contributed by Christine Labagh, San Francisco, CA, Summer 2004.

How Else Can We Use This Strategy?

Group Mode: The guide is displayed on chart paper, a board, or an overhead transparency. Statements are presented orally and students invited to share their reactions and opinions. A group recorder tallies "agree" and "disagree" responses.

Changing Opinions: Students write whether they agree or disagree with a statement in the left margin of the paper. They then fold under the left side of the paper so they cannot see it. Later, after they have read the selection, they make new decisions about the statements and note those decisions in the right margin. Finally, they compare their opinions and note whether any have changed.

Fictional Characters: Before students begin reading, they note their opinions about teacher-written statements. After reading, they note how they think a particular character in the literature would feel about the same statements.

Where Can We Learn More?

Duffelmeyer, F. A. (1994). Effective anticipation guide statements for learning from expository prose. *Journal of Reading, 37,* 452–457.

Head, M. H., & Readence, J. E. (1992). Anticipation guides: Using prediction to promote meaning through text. In E. K. Dishner, T. W. Bean, J. E. Readence, & D. W. Moore (Eds.), *Reading in the content areas: Improving classroom instruction* (3rd ed., pp. 27–233). Dubuque, IA: Kendall/Hunt.

McLaughlin, M., & Allen, M. B. (2002). *Guided comprehension: A teaching model for grades 3–8.* Newark: International Reading Association.

Merkley, D. J. (1997). Modified anticipation guide. In Rasinski, T. V. et al. (Eds.), *Teaching comprehension and exploring multiple literacies: Strategies from the Reading Teacher* (pp. 59–63.). Newark, DE: International Reading Association.

Tompkins, G. E. (2004). *Fifty literacy strategies: Step by step* (2nd ed.). Upper Saddle River, NJ: Prentice Hall.

Wood, K. D. (2001). *Literacy strategies across the subject areas.* Needham Heights, MA: Allyn & Bacon.

Yopp, R. H., & Yopp, H. K. (2001). *Literature-based reading activities* (3rd ed.). Boston: Allyn & Bacon.

3

Bio Poem

> Also Called: Name Poem, Character Poetry
>
> Suggested Grade Levels: 3 to 8
>
> Elements Addressed: Character
>
> Meta-Strategies Incorporated: Making connections, making inferences, summarizing and synthesizing
>
> Supplies: Any text with a strong central character, bio poem worksheet or lined paper and handout with bio poem formula, pens or pencils

WHAT IS A BIO POEM? ●

A bio poem is a creative piece of writing assigned to facilitate analysis of a character.

When Do We Use It?

This strategy is best used after students have finished reading a novel or a story or after they have studied a nonfiction character.

Why Do We Use It?

To write a bio poem, a student must develop an understanding of the subject, whether a literary character or a famous person. This requires analyzing the text to build comprehension.

How Do We Use Bio Poems?

After students have finished reading a story or a nonfiction selection (or have finished listening to a story), the teacher distributes a handout with the formula printed on it. The teacher discusses the formula as well as the notion of word choice and the role of words in poetry. To model, the teacher leads the class in writing the first bio poem on the board as a group.

After the group has worked together on a poem, students have the opportunity to write their own poem. They may select another character from the same piece of literature to serve as a subject, or they may use the formula after reading something new. After they complete their work, students may share what they have written orally, or the teacher may post the poems around the room.

To write the poem, students use this formula:

Line 1: Character's first name

Line 2: Title given to the character

Line 3: Four words that describe the character

Line 4: "Lover of [three things, objects, or ideas]"

Line 5: "Who believed [one idea or concept]"

Line 6: "Who wanted [three things]"

Line 7: "Who used [three things]"

Line 8: "Who gave [three things]"

Line 9: "Who said [direct quote]"

Line 10: Character's last name or a synonymous descriptor

How Else Can We Use This Strategy?

Me Poem: Students write bio poems about themselves. Having students write "Me poems" prior to writing bio poems is a good idea because most students can describes themselves more easily than they can describe a character.

Where Can We Learn More?

McLaughlin, M., & Allen, B. A. (2002). *Guided comprehension: A teaching model for grades 3–8.* Newark, DE: International Reading Association.

Morrie, Y., & Simmons, B. (1995). Explorer "bio poem." *School Library Media Activities Monthly, 11,* 35.

Schulz, A. R. (1998). Bio-poems: A creative response scaffold. In *Supporting intermediate and secondary readers: Selected interactive approaches for grades 4–12* (pp. 6–10). Costa Mesa: CA: California Reading Association.

Figure 3.1

Bio Poem

Your Name _____

Title of Book _____

Line 1: **Character's first name**

_____

Line 2: **Title given to the character**

_____

Line 3: **Four words that describe the character**

_____   _____   _____   _____

Line 4: **"Lover of [three things, objects, or ideas]"**

_____   _____   _____

Line 5: **"Who believed [one idea or concept]"**

_____

Line 6: **"Who wanted [three things]"**

_____   _____   _____

Line 7: **"Who used [three things]"**

_____   _____   _____

Line 8: **"Who gave [three things]"**

_____   _____   _____

Line 9: **"Who said [direct quote]"**

_____

Line 10: **Character's last name, or synonym that describes him/her**

_____

Figure 3.2

BIO POEM

Goldilocks

Wanderer of the woods

Curious, selfish, hungry, careless

Lover of snooping, things that aren't hers, and making a mess

Who believed that she was entitled to anything she wanted

Who wanted a snack, a place to sit, and somewhere to take a nap

Who used hot porridge, chairs, and beds that were not hers

Who gave zilch, zero, nothing

Who screamed, "Ahhh! A Bear!"

Young girl who was never seen in the woods again

Contributed by Amanda Rawls, San Francisco, CA, Fall 2003.

Figure 3.3   Sample bio poem based on *Roll of Thunder, Hear my Cry*

BIO POEM

Based on *Roll of Thunder, Hear my Cry*

Uncle Hammer

Hammer

Uncle of three children

Bold, short-tempered, standoutish, strong-willed

Lover of equality, fairness, family

Who believed in freedom

Who wanted blacks and whites to be treated equal

Who drove a fancy silver Packard car just like Mr. Granger's

Who gave Stacey a new winter coat

And gave his time and energy to his family

Who dreamed that someday everyone would be judged by their inside

And not by the color of their skin

Who said, "You think my brother died

And I got my leg cut off in the German war

To have some red-neck knock Cassie around anytime it suits him?"

Logan

Book used: Taylor, M. (1997). Roll of Thunder, Hear my Cry. East Rutherford, NJ Penguin/ Puffin Books.

Contributed by Katie B., grade 5, San Francisco, CA, Summer 2003.

Book Box

Suggested Grade Levels: 3 to 8

Elements Addressed: Plot/theme

Meta-Strategies Incorporated: Making connections, making inferences (predicting)

Supplies: Narrative or expository text, a box (or some other container, such as a can, basket, or bag), lined paper, pens or pencils, three to five objects related to the book or story

WHAT IS A BOOK BOX? ●

A book box is a container of some sort with several objects in it related to a book.

When Do We Use It?

Book boxes made by a teacher are effective when presented before the class begins reading. Students might create book boxes or book bags to end a literature unit after reading a book.

Why Do We Use It?

Teachers use book boxes to introduce a new piece of literature and to help students build background knowledge, including knowledge of vocabulary and story themes. Based on the objects the teacher has selected, students predict what might happen in a story. After discussing the items presented by the teacher, students often focus on their reading to learn how the objects are really related.

Students make personal connections to the text when they create book boxes and bags at the end of a literature unit. The project engages the interest of all students, regardless of reading ability.

How Do We Use Book Boxes?

Before the class begins reading a book, the teacher pre-reads it and makes a list of several objects that might represent themes in the book. Next, the teacher finds a box, a basket, a tub, a bag, or some other container to use as the "box"; writes the name of the book on the container; and decorates it with pictures related to the story. Then the teacher gathers three to five objects from the list and places them in the container.

The teacher introduces the activity by letting students know that each object in the container represents something important in the selected reading. As each object is held up, students identify it. They then speculate about how it might be important to the book and predict what might happen. After each student has had an opportunity to share an idea and all have had a chance to respond to each other, the teacher selects a second object from the container, and the activity is repeated. Students may make connections between the second and first objects and may have new ideas about the first object. They may also change their original prediction altogether. Each time a new item is introduced, the process is repeated.

Before students begin reading, the teacher instructs them to watch for the objects discussed and to think about how accurate their predictions were.

How Else Can We Use This Strategy?

Student Book Boxes: Students create their own boxes after reading a book. To do this, they must think carefully about important ideas within the story and about objects that might represent those ideas. They then share their boxes with the rest of the class, explaining the relevance of each item.

Book Bags: Students decorate the front of a paper lunch bag with a book's title, author, and related images. They may also decorate the back and sides of the bag. Next, they collect five objects related to the text and place them in the bag, along with a copy of the text. Students may also include an inventory sheet listing the items and their relevance. They present their book bags and rationales orally to the class. After all students have presented their bags, teachers may hold a "gallery walk" so that the class can look more closely at all of the objects.

Story Retelling: Students create their own book box after reading independently. They then tell the story to the rest of the class, sharing the objects they have selected as they speak.

Where Can We Learn More?

Tompkins, G. E. (2003). *Literacy for the twenty-first century: A balanced approach* (3rd ed.). Upper Saddle River, NJ: Merrill/Prentice Hall.

Tompkins, G. E. (2004). *Fifty literacy strategies: Step by step* (2nd ed.). Upper Saddle River, NJ: Pearson-Prentice Hall.

Yopp, R. H., & Yopp, H. K. (2001). *Literature-based reading activities* (3rd ed.). Boston: Allyn & Bacon.

Figure 4.1

Alice's Book Box

Artifacts to represent the White Rabbit in
Alice's Adventures in Wonderland

<u>Chapter 1:</u>

- **Watch**
- **Waistcoat pocket (sewn from scrap cloth)**
- **Orange marmalade**
- **Golden key**

<u>Chapter 2:</u>

- **White kid gloves**
- **Fan**

<u>Chapter 7:</u>

- **Tea set (miniature)**

<u>Chapter 9:</u>

- **Trumpet (plastic toy)**
- **Scroll paper**

Book used: Carroll, L. (1865/1960). *Alice's adventures in wonderland and through the looking glass.* New York: Penguin Putnam.

Contributed by Caryn Barry, Jenn Jurcy, and Tobi Slavet, San Francisco, CA, Summer 2004.

5

Brainstorming

> Suggested Grade Levels: K to 8
>
> Elements Addressed: Plot/theme, character, expository text
>
> Meta-Strategies Incorporated: Determining important information, summarizing and synthesizing
>
> Supplies: Narrative or expository text, a large board or flipchart, dark-colored markers

● WHAT IS BRAINSTORMING?

Brainstorming is a strategy used within groups to generate many new and useful ideas.

When Do We Use It?

Brainstorming may be used as an opening activity to trigger students' existing knowledge about a topic before they begin reading. It invites students to tell all they know about a particular topic or idea and helps them think about what might occur in a story or prepares them for an expository reading. The technique may also be used after students have finished reading but before they begin writing.

Why Do We Use It?

Through brainstorming, students discover a wide range of ideas. As they listen to one idea, they think of others and come up with fresh, new ways of thinking about things. The activity usually generates many ideas about a given subject.

Teachers also engage students in brainstorming before they begin reading to find out what students already know about a topic.

How Do We Use Brainstorming?

Before this activity begins, the teacher chooses several questions to start discussion about a book or a section of a book. The questions should be open-ended, encouraging students to think about the reading and to apply concepts to their personal experiences. They can relate to the story's plot, theme, characters, or setting or even to the author.

For groups of younger students, the teacher serves as the recorder, noting ideas on the board or flipchart. For older children, one student is selected to record ideas.

The teacher instructs students to respond to questions as they like but to keep responses brief. Students are told that there is no one correct answer to the questions. All ideas are welcomed; none are rejected. Students do not need to raise their hands but should take turns speaking. When one student finishes, another may jump in with a different response or with a reaction to the first student's comment. The goal is to offer the recorder as many ideas as possible about the subject at hand.

The first question is read and a volunteer requested. If no one volunteers, the teacher selects a student and asks what the person thinks. The recorder takes notes as students speak. In the case of silence, the teacher may call on a specific student for a response or may go on to another question.

How Else Can We Use This Strategy?

Round Robin: The recorder asks each group member in turn for an idea and then records the idea. Group members may pass if they like. The round continues until each group member has spoken or passed.

Slip Method: Instead of speaking, students write their ideas on small pieces of paper. The recorder then collects and organizes the ideas before writing them down.

Clustering the Brainstormed Ideas: The teacher or recorder helps students create an organized visual representation of ideas (a "cluster") that can be viewed graphically. Clustering helps get ideas flowing on a given topic. The recorder writes a keyword or phrase in the center of a circle and draws lines outward from the circle (like the rays on a child's illustration of the sun) to show radiating ideas. All words are encircled, with lines linking ideas that are related to each other. As brainstorming progresses, the recorder draws lines projecting from each circle to accommodate additional ideas as they are offered. Clustering is a nonlinear brainstorming process akin to free association.

Clustering can be especially useful for determining relationships between ideas. With it, students are able to distinguish how ideas fit together, especially with an abundance of ideas. Clustering lets everyone see the brainstormed ideas visually in a different way, enabling students to more readily understand possible links and relationships.

The Pre-Reading Plan (PREP): PREP is a version of brainstorming developed by Judith Langer (1982) to give students a way to consider information before reading. It can be done as a whole class or in directed small-group discussions. PREP begins with the teacher saying, "Tell me anything that comes to your mind when I say _____ (e.g., 'pigs' or 'spiders' or 'farms')." The students' free associations are recorded on the board. The teacher next points to a response on the board and asks, "What made you think of _____ (each student's response to the first statement)?" After responses have been clarified and elaborated, the teacher says, "On the basis of our discussion, do you have any new ideas about (e.g., 'pigs' or 'spiders' or 'farms')?" The new responses may also be recorded. Finally, after all discussion, students read the story (or expository text) to see how their old and new ideas apply.

Where Can We Learn More?

Bromley, K. (1996). *Webbing with literature: Creating story maps with children's books.* Boston: Allyn & Bacon.

Cooper, J. D. (2006). *Literacy: Helping children construct meaning* (6th ed.). Boston: Houghton Mifflin.

Idol, L. (1987). Group story mapping: A comprehension strategy for both skilled and unskilled readers. *Journal of Learning Disabilities, 20*(4), 196–205.

Langer, J. (1982). Facilitating text processing: The elaboration of prior knowledge. In J. A. Langer & M. T. Smith-Burke (Eds.), *Reader meets author/bridging the gap* (pp. 149–162). Newark, DE: International Reading Association.

Rico, G. L. (1983). *Writing the natural way.* Los Angeles: Tarcher.

Sorrell, A. L. (1990). Three reading comprehension strategies: TELLS, story mapping, and QARs. *Academic Therapy, 25*(3), 359–368.

Figure 5.1

Cluster Generated Through Brainstorming

(Based on *Sylvester and the Magic Pebble*)

To initiate brainstorming, the teacher asked students the question, "What happened to Sylvester in the story?"

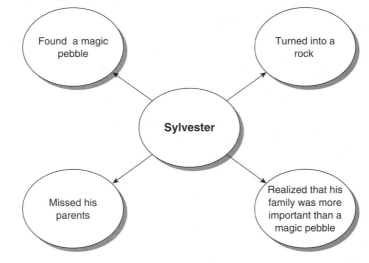

Book used: Steig, W. (1969). *Sylvester and the magic pebble.* New York: Aladdin Paperbacks, Simon & Schuster.

Contributed by Kate Working, San Francisco, CA, Fall 2003.

Figure 5.2

Cluster Generated Through Brainstorming

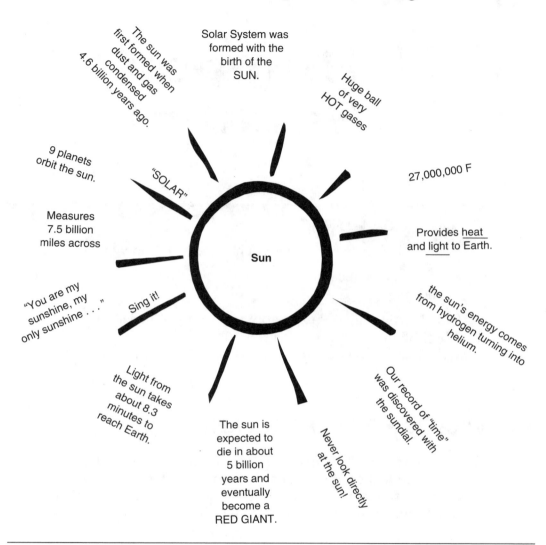

Contributed by Eliza Lurie, San Francisco, CA, Fall 2003.

6

Bumper Stickers

Suggested Grade Levels: 3 to 8

Elements Addressed: Plot/theme, character, expository text

Meta-Strategies Incorporated: Making inferences, summarizing and synthesizing

Supplies: Narrative or expository text, strips of paper approximately 4 by 11.5 inches, markers; pads of sticky notes

● WHAT IS A BUMPER STICKER?

A "bumper sticker" is a slip of paper on which is written a slogan or a saying that a student creates to summarize a character or a theme in a piece of literature. The saying may instead be a quotation taken directly from the reading to summarize a key idea about a character or concept.

When Do We Use It?

This strategy may be used in the middle of reading or after students have completed an entire selection.

Why Do We Use It?

To create a slogan, students must interpret text using both prior knowledge and personal experience. The activity also encourages students to find the underlying meaning or moral of a story or character. When students create the slogan or saying for their bumper sticker, they summarize what they have learned and inferred from their reading. To create the slogan, they also must synthesize what they know or have learned.

How Do We Use Bumper Stickers?

Before this activity begins, the teacher identifies some concept or aspect of the reading to be summarized. For example, students may focus on a specific character or on a theme, lesson, moral, or truth of the story.

The teacher explains the activity to students. After introducing the focus, she or he gives some examples of possible slogans or quotations to represent the idea. Students then create original slogans in response to the concept introduced. Alternatively, they choose a quote, sentence, or phrase from the text to best summarize the concept or character. They write their slogan or quote on a slip of paper and illustrate with graphics. Creativity is encouraged for this activity.

The teacher may ask students to write a few sentences on the back of their bumper sticker to explain the reasoning behind the expression they have chosen.

After all bumper stickers have been created, they can be posted around the room. Students have the opportunity to respond by writing comments on sticky notes and attaching them to the bumper stickers.

Figure 6.1

Bumper Sticker

Based on the Book *Oliver Button Is a Sissy*

OLIVER BUTTON IS A
~~SISSY~~ STAR!

Book Synopsis: Oliver Button is a little boy who likes to play dress up, take walks in the wood, and dance. Oliver's father wants him to be less of a sissy, and the boys at school tease Oliver for acting like a girl. Oliver, however, stays true to himself and enters a talent show where he tap dances. The book provides a great opportunity for young children to explore gender roles.

Book used: DePaolo, T. (1990). *Oliver Button is a sissy.* Orlando, FL: Voyager Books, Harcourt Brace.

Contributed by Kate Working, San Francisco, CA, Fall 2003.

How Else Can We Use This Strategy?

Personal Significance: Instead of providing a concept for focus, the teacher instructs students to choose a phrase or sentence that is especially significant to them. Discussion follows.

Buttons: Students create buttons instead of bumper stickers.

Graffiti: Students write their slogans or quotes on a large piece of butcher paper taped to the classroom wall.

Character Slogans: Students create slogans or copy quotes to represent a chosen character but do not write the name of the character on the paper. Other students guess which bumper sticker belongs to which character.

Where Can We Learn More?

California Literature Project. Retrieved July 7, 2004, from www.memorial.sdcs.
    k12.ca.us/LESSONS/LaLloronaUnit/ronatg2.html

Farris, P., Fuhler, C., & Walther, M. (2004). *Teaching reading: A balanced approach for
    today's classrooms.* New York: McGraw-Hill.

Lapp, D., Fisher, D., & Flood, J. (1999). Integrating the language arts and content
    areas: Effective research-based strategies. *The California Reader, 32*(4), 35–38.

Whitin, P. E. (1994). Opening potential: Visual response to literature. *Language
    Arts, 7*(2), 101–107.

7

Central Story Problem

> Suggested Grade Levels: K to 5
>
> Elements Addressed: Plot/theme
>
> Meta-Strategies Incorporated: Monitoring reading for meaning (clarifying), determining important information, making inferences, summarizing and synthesizing
>
> Supplies: Any text with a strong story line, a board or flipchart, dark-colored markers, story problem worksheet or lined paper, pens or pencils

WHAT IS A CENTRAL STORY PROBLEM?

A central story problem is the main problem, or conflict, in a piece of literature.

When Do We Use It?

Students are introduced to this strategy before they begin to read a selection. They complete the assignment after they have finished reading.

Why Do We Use It?

This strategy helps students understand the concept of a main problem, or conflict, within a story. Students also see how different elements relate to the problem.

How Do We Use Central Story Problems?

Students may use this strategy as independent seatwork, but some preliminary teacher direction and modeling are first necessary.

To introduce the central story problem, the teacher directs students to listen for who, where, when, and what happens (events) in a story that is read aloud. After the story is read, students share the information they have collected, and the teacher records it on the chalkboard, chart, or overhead projector.

Next, the class discusses the idea of "problems," or story conflicts. Students are invited to share personal problems, such as a lost pet, ruined homework, a family accident, and so on. The teacher explains that stories also have problems, or conflicts. The events of the story relate to that problem and its solution. Children are encouraged to think about the *who, where, when,* and *what* information they have noted. Then volunteers offer ideas about what the main problem in the story is and how it is solved. The teacher records this information as the class together completes the central story problem form.

After students are familiar with the procedure, they may use it to summarize stories they read on their own. They are reminded to first think about who, where, when, and what happens. Next, they are to identify the central story problem, referring to their notes. On their worksheet or in their literature response logs, they complete the two sentences, "At the beginning of the story, the problem starts when . . ." and "At the end of the story, the problem is solved when . . ." For older students, a third sentence may be added: "In the middle of the story, the character faces these roadblocks in trying to solve the problem . . ."

How Else Can We Use This Strategy?

Mapping Variation: Students begin by mapping who, where, when, and what happens in the story. They then complete the sentences about the start and resolution of the problem.

Where Can We Learn More?

Idol, L. (1987). Group story mapping: A comprehension strategy for both skilled and unskilled readers. *Journal of Learning Disabilities, 20*(4), 196–205.

Hennings, D. G. (2002). *Communication in action: Teaching literature-based language arts* (8th ed.). Boston: Houghton Mifflin.

Tompkins, G. E. (1998). *Language arts: Content and teaching strategies* (4th ed.). Upper Saddle River, NJ: Prentice Hall.

Figure 7.1

What's the **Problem**?

Story Title: _____

Who is the main character? _____

Where does the story take place? _____

When does the story take place? _____

What happens in the story?

_____

_____

_____

_____

The main **problem** in the story is . . .

_____

At the beginning of the story, the **problem** <u>starts</u> when . . .

_____

At the end of the story, the **problem** is <u>solved</u> when . . .

Copyright © 2006 by Corwin Press. All rights reserved. Reprinted from *60 Strategies for Improving Reading Comprehension in Grades K – 8*, by Kathleen Feeney Jonson. Thousand Oaks, CA: Corwin Press, www.corwinpress.com. Reproduction authorized only for the local school site that has purchased this book.

8

Character Bag

Suggested Grade Levels: 3 to 8

Elements Addressed: Character

Meta-Strategies Incorporated: Summarizing and synthesizing

Supplies: Narrative text, one lunch-size paper bag per student, white or colored drawing paper, markers, scissors, glue, miscellaneous items to represent characters

• WHAT IS A CHARACTER BAG?

A character bag is a container and a collection of items that represent a character.

When Do We Use It?

Students create a character bag while they are reading or after they have completed the text. Either they can start the bag early on and add to it as they learn more about a character, or they can create the bag as a summary activity after reading.

Why Do We Use It?

When students create a character bag, they synthesize their knowledge of a character. Students use both direct and inferred information to determine the contents of the bag.

How Do We Use Character Bags?

To begin this activity—either after a section of reading or after the complete text has been read—the teacher gives each student a bag and instructs students to choose a character to be represented. Students then cover the outside of the bag with quotes, symbols, and artwork to represent the character, being as creative as they would like. Next, they think about objects that represent the character to be put in the bag, drawing on both direct information and inferences about the character. For example, a small book might represent a character who loves to read; a toy dog might symbolize one with a favorite pet; a stick of gum might symbolize a gum chewer. Students include quotes explaining the connection between each object and the character.

Where Can We Learn More?

Emery, D. (1996). Helping readers comprehend stories from the characters' perspectives. *The Reading Teacher, 49,* 534–541.

Yopp, H. K., & Yopp, R. H. (1996). *Literature-based reading activities* (2nd ed.). Boston: Allyn & Bacon

Figure 8.1   Character Bag Based on *Wemberly Worried*

Book used: Hendes, K. (2000). *Wemberly Worried*. New York: Greenwillow Books.

9

Character Mapping

Also Called: Character Web

Suggested Grade Levels: 3 to 8

Elements Addressed: Character

Meta-Strategies Incorporated: Visualizing, making inferences, summarizing and synthesizing

Supplies: Narrative text, drawing paper, pencils or markers

● WHAT IS A CHARACTER MAP?

A character map is a visual organizer used to display personality traits of a specific character.

When Do We Use It?

Character mapping is most effective when done after an entire book has been read. It can be used as preparation for a writing activity.

Why Do We Use It?

This strategy helps students think about a character's traits. Because many of these traits are not described explicitly in the text, students are forced to infer important characteristics. The strategy is particularly useful for the many students who think better visually than through text alone.

How Do We Use Character Mapping?

After students complete their reading, the teacher instructs them to draw a circle or another shape in the middle of their paper and then draw a picture of a character or write the character's name in the center of the shape. Students next draw lines extending from the shape. At the end of each line, students record a personality trait of the character, such as "courageous," "resourceful," "responsible," or "loyal." They can then draw another line extending from the character trait. At the end of this line, students record actions in the story (evidence) that support the personality trait. Alternatively, they may record a quote from the character or draw a picture or symbol related to the character.

This activity works particularly well in small cooperative learning groups. Students discuss the characters and select traits most important for representation. Because many traits must be inferred, students are forced to think about the character's actions in the book.

For children in primary grades, extra teacher direction and assistance are needed throughout the activity.

Figure 9.1   Character Map

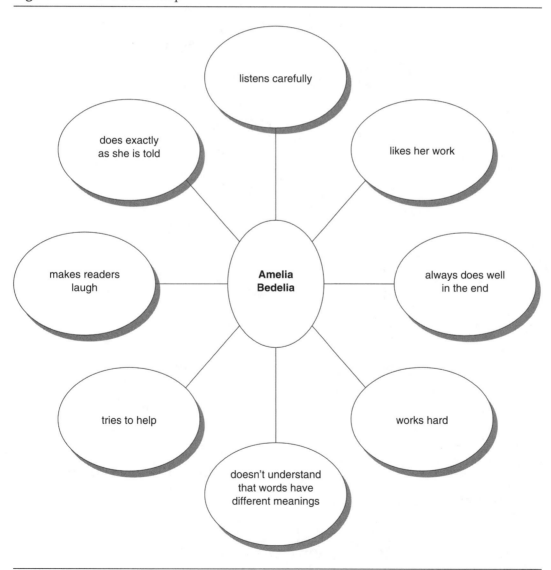

Book used: Parish, P., & Siebel F. (1963). *Amelia Bedelia*. New York: Harper Trophy.

Figure 9.2 Character Map

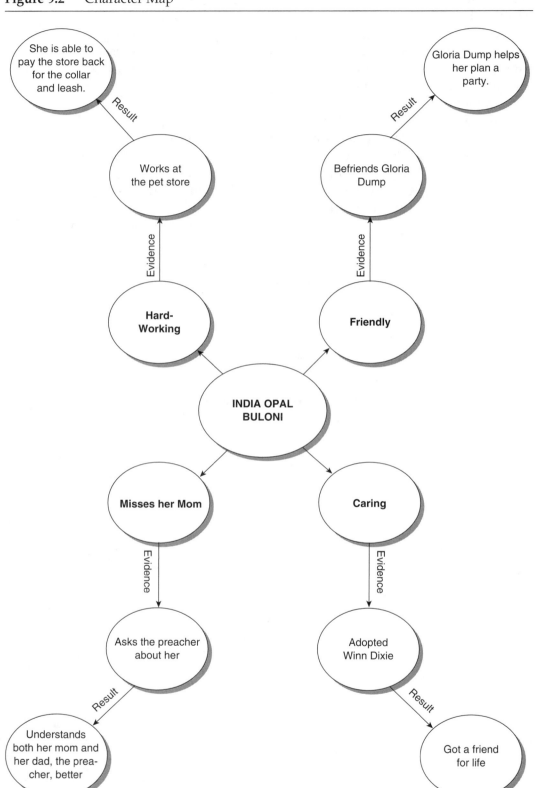

Book used: Dicamillo, K. (2000). *Because of Winn Dixie*. Cambridge, Mass: Candlewick Press.

Contributed by: Kate Working, San Francisco, CA. Fall 2003.

Figure 9.3 Character Map Template

Character Map

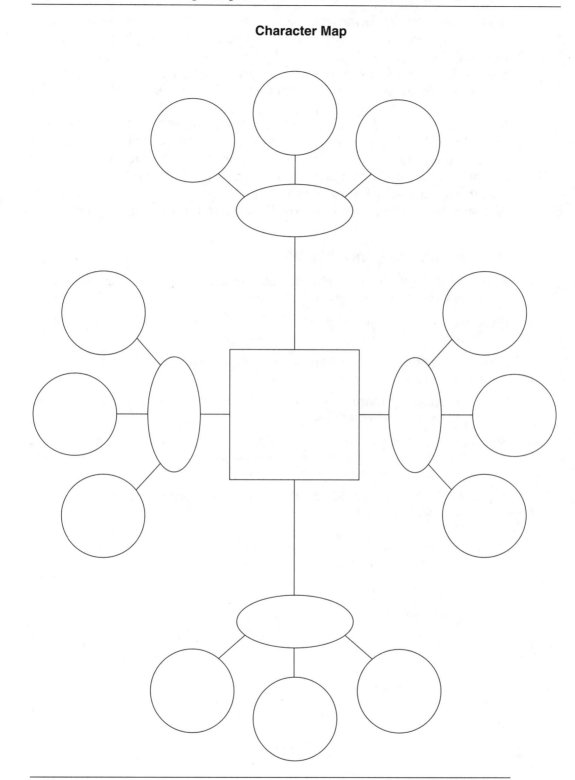

Copyright © 2006 by Corwin Press. All rights reserved. Reprinted from *60 Strategies for Improving Reading Comprehension in Grades K – 8,* by Kathleen Feeney Jonson. Thousand Oaks, CA: Corwin Press, www.corwinpress.com. Reproduction authorized only for the local school site that has purchased this book.

How Else Can We Use This Strategy?

Evidence and Results: Students create three levels of mapping, with the character in the center. In the first level of mapping, students write words that describe the character. In the second level, students give evidence of those traits—things that happened in the book to indicate the trait. Finally, a third level is added for the recording of results, or consequences, of those traits.

Literary Report Cards: First, students assess the merits and faults of a character through mapping, placing all faults on one side, linked, and merits on the other. Then students create a "report card," grading the character on various personality traits, such as "patience," "responsibility," "respect for others," and so on. Younger students can assign characters "excellent," "satisfactory," or "needs to improve" marks rather than letter grades.

Where Can We Learn More?

Bluestein, N. A. (2002). Comprehension through characterization: Enabling readers to make personal connections with literature. *Reading Teacher, 55*(5), 431–434.

Bromley, K. (1996). *Webbing with literature: Creating story maps with children's books.* Boston: Allyn & Bacon.

Emery, D. (1996). Helping readers comprehend stories from the characters' perspectives. *The Reading Teacher 49,* 534–541.

Fink, L. S. *Mapping characters across book series.* Retrieved March 3, 2005, from http://www.readwritethink.org/lessons

Shanahan, T., & Shanahan, S. (1997). Character perspective charting: Helping children to develop a more complete conception of story. *The Reading Teacher, 50,* 668–677.

Yopp, R. H., & Yopp, H. K. (2001). *Literature-based reading activities* (3rd ed.). Boston: Allyn & Bacon.

10

Creating Chapter Titles

Suggested Grade Levels: 3 to 8

Elements Addressed: Plot/theme, character, expository text

Meta-Strategies Incorporated: Determining important information, summarizing and synthesizing

Supplies: Any book without chapter titles in it; lined paper; pens or pencils

WHAT IS CREATING CHAPTER TITLES?

Chapter titles often express the main idea or theme of a section of text. In this strategy, students create or write their own titles for chapters.

When Do We Use It?

Students create titles immediately after reading each relevant section of text.

Why Do We Use It?

This strategy forces students to focus on important concepts within a section and to think critically about what has happened. It requires students to synthesize the material from the section and determine the main point.

How Do We Use Creating Chapter Titles?

Before beginning this strategy, the class discusses sample chapter books that have chapter titles, such as the books from the *Harry Potter* series. Students explore the novels, analyzing chapter titles to see if there is a pattern, logic, or sequence to them and noting any other characteristics of the titles. The teacher may ask questions to guide exploration. For example,

- How does the chapter title relate to the chapter content?
- Is there anything special or significant about the chapter title?
- What is the grammatical structure of the chapter title?
- What stands out about the word choice in the chapter title?

Next, after reading a section of text—a chapter, a chapter section, or a page—students determine the main idea and create a title of their own for the section. Students may work individually, in pairs, or in small groups. They must think about all of the things that happen in the section and figure out the main point. After they have chosen a title, they share their idea with the larger group and explain their rationale for choosing that title.

This activity works especially well with books that do not have chapter titles. Alternatively, students may choose titles other than the author's originals or come up with titles for sections within chapters.

How Else Can We Use This Strategy?

Read-Aloud Books for Younger Children: Younger children listen to a story read aloud and then choose a title for the book.

Parts of Speech: Students create titles in the *noun-verb* pattern (e.g., "Sarah Came"), in the *adjective-noun* pattern (e.g., "The Violent Wind"), or ending with a particular *suffix* (e.g., "Realization," "Indecision," "Creation"). Teachers may use this variation to review parts of speech.

Where Can We Learn More?

Broida, E. (1995). Name that chapter! *Teaching Literature in High School: The Novel,* pp. 41–42. Urbana, IL: National Council of Teachers of English.

Gardner, T. (2002). *Name that chapter! Discussing summary and interpretation using chapter titles.* Retrieved March 3, 2005, from http://www.readwritethink.org/lessons

Hennings, D., & McCreesh, G. (1994). Titling: Finding names that "mean." *The Reading Teacher, 48*(October), 186–187.

Lubliner, S. (2001). Terrific titles. In S. Lubliner (Ed), *A practical guide to reciprocal teaching* (pp. 44–45, 141). Bothell, WA: Wright Group/McGraw-Hill.

Suggested Books to Use to Create Chapter Titles

DiCamillo, K. (2001). *Because of Winn-Dixie.* Cambridge, MA: Candlewick.

Konigsburg, E. (1968). *From the mixed-up files of Mrs. Basil E. Frankweiler.* New York: Atheneum.

MacLachlan, P. (1985). *Sarah, plain and tall.* New York: HarperCollins.

Odell, S. *The Island of the blue dolphins.* Boston, MA: Houghton.

Paterson, K. (1980). *Jacob, have I loved.* New York: Crowell.

Paulson, G. (1988). *Hatchet.* New York: Puffin Books.

Scieszka, J. (1991) *The not-so-jolly Roger.* New York: Puffin Books.

Sachar, L. (1999). *Holes.* New York: Frances Foster Books.

Snicket, L. (1999). *The reptile room.* New York: HarperCollins.

Snicket, L. (2000). *The wide window.* New York: HarperCollins.

Taylor, M. (1976). *Roll of thunder, hear my cry.* New York: Dial.

11

Crossword Puzzle

> Suggested Grade Levels: 6 to 8
>
> Elements Addressed: Plot/theme, character, expository text
>
> Meta-Strategies Incorporated: Monitoring reading for meaning, asking questions, summarizing and synthesizing
>
> Supplies: Narrative or expository text, graph paper with large squares, lined paper, pencils

● WHAT IS THE CROSSWORD PUZZLE ACTIVITY?

To create a crossword puzzle, students select important words from a text, write definitions or clues for them, and design their own puzzle.

When Do We Use It?

Students create a crossword puzzle after completing their reading.

Why Do We Use It?

Creating a crossword puzzle encourages students to review the material they have read to choose key concepts. They must think about the meaning of concepts or the traits of characters they have selected to briefly define the terms. The activity allows for creativity in working with words.

How Do We Use the Crossword Puzzle Activity?

After students complete their reading, they review the material and jot down twelve to twenty keywords. The words may be character names, place names, or key concepts from the book. Next, students write simple definitions or clues for the words.

Students use the graph paper to create a crossword puzzle based on the words, writing the letters in the squares. They then number the words, starting in the upper left corner, moving to the right, then moving back to the left for the next word down, and so on. After they have arranged and numbered all of the words, they outline the boxes on a separate piece of graph paper and fill in the numbers but not the words. Definitions or clues are numbered and written—under the headings of "Across" and "Down"—on a separate sheet of paper.

Students trade their work with a partner and practice with the crossword puzzles.

How Else Can We Use This Strategy?

Word Search: Younger children choose keywords or concepts and arrange them in a word search.

Where Can We Learn More?

Haggard, M. R. (1986). The vocabulary self-collection strategy: Using student interest and world knowledge to enhance vocabulary growth. *Journal of Reading, 29,* 634–642.

Oczkus, L. (2004). Word Puzzles. In *Super six comprehension strategies: Thirty-five lessons and more for reading success* (pp. 161–163). Norwood, MA: Christopher-Gordon.

Schwartz, R. M., & Raphael, T. Concept of definition: A key to improving students' vocabulary. *The Reading Teacher, 39,* 198–205.

Figure 11.1

Crossword Puzzle

Based on *Harry Potter and the Order of the Phoenix*

Down

1. A magical powder that gives you boils.

2. The first password to get into Gryffindor tower.

5. A spell you can use to read someone's thoughts and memories.

7. Someone who can change his or her appearance at will.

9. Professor Grubbly-Plank's first name.

10. A member of the Order of the Phoenix. She is an Auror and a Metamorphmagus. Her first name is Nymphadora.

11. A Hufflepuff boy with an attitude. He plays on the Hufflepuff Quidditch team. His last name is Smith.

Across

3. A newspaper for witches or wizards (Luna's dad is the editor).

4. The charm to lock doors (the opposite of Alohomora).

6. Horselike animals that look like skeletons. They have blank white staring eyes. You can only see them if you have watched somebody die. They pull the school carriages.

8. Creatures that live in mistletoe.

12. The author of *Defensive Magical Theory.* His first name is Wilbert.

13. He is the Quidditch hero for Bulgaria. His last name is Krum.

(Continued)

Figure 11.1 (Continued)

Key:

Down: 1. Bulbadox Powder   2. Mimbulus Mimbletonia   5. Legilimens   7. Metamorphmagus
          9. Wilhelmina   10. Tonks   11. Zacharias

Across: 3. Quibbler   4. Collopartus   6. Thestral   8. Nargles   12. Slinkhard   13. Viktor

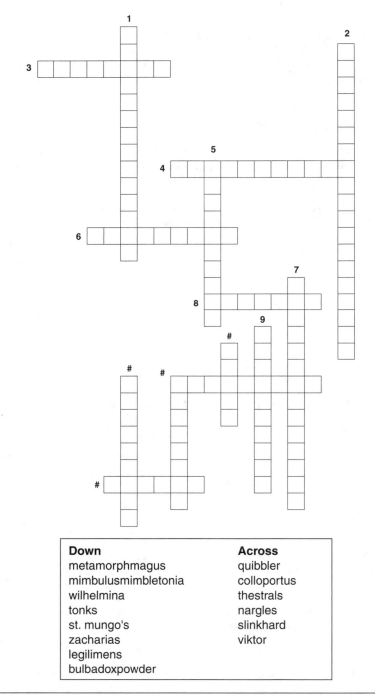

***Harry Potter and the Order
of the Phoenix
J. K. Rowling***

Down	Across
metamorphmagus	quibbler
mimbulusmimbletonia	colloportus
wilhelmina	thestrals
tonks	nargles
st. mungo's	slinkhard
zacharias	viktor
legilimens	
bulbadoxpowder	

Book used: Rowling, J. K. (2003). *Harry Potter and the order of the phoenix.* New York: Scholastic.
Contributed by Alicia Fuller, Concord, CA, Spring 2005.

12

Cubing

Suggested Grade Levels: 3 to 8

Elements Addressed: Plot/theme, expository text

Meta-Strategies Incorporated: Summarizing and synthesizing

Supplies: Any text with strong thematic or informational content, drawing paper, pens or pencils

WHAT IS CUBING? ●

Cubing is an activity in which students think about a topic or theme in six different ways: they describe it, compare it, analyze it, associate it, apply it, and argue for or against it. The activity is called "cubing" because of the six dimensions involved, corresponding to the six sides of a cube.

When Do We Use It?

Cubing is used after completion of a reading unit or informational study.

Why Do We Use It?

This strategy forces students to focus on different aspects of a topic.

How Do We Use Cubing?

The first time this strategy is used, the teacher assigns a topic for cubing. If the strategy is used more than once, older students may choose their own topic for subsequent activities. This strategy is particularly effective for thematic units, such as a study of the Civil War, pollution, or technology development.

The teacher leads a discussion of the six different ways of viewing a topic or theme:

1. Describe it. What does the thing look like? What color, shape, and size is it?

2. Compare it. How is the thing similar to or different from something else?

3. Analyze it. What is the thing made of?

4. Associate it. What does the thing make you think about? Why?

5. Apply it. How can it be used? What can be done with it?

6. Argue for or against it. What is your stand on the issue? Why?

Next, students are divided into six groups, and each group is assigned responsibility for one dimension. Students in the group brainstorm about their dimension and then assign one group leader to write about that dimension. After all students have completed their writing, they share with the class. Finally, all six writings are collected and attached to the sides of a cube.

How Else Can We Use This Strategy?

Group Cubes: The class may be broken into groups of six students each. Groups then choose their own topics. Each student within the group is responsible for writing about one dimension of the topic, and all writings are assembled on a cube.

Character Cube: Students may make a cube about a character in a piece of literature, using variations on the six dimensions.

Where Can We Learn More?

McLaughlin, M., & Allen, M. B. (2002). *Guided Comprehension: A teaching model for grades 3–8.* Newark: International Reading Association.

Tompkins, G. E. (2004). *Fifty literacy strategies: Step by step* (2nd ed.). Upper Saddle River, NJ: Prentice Hall.

Figure 12.1   Cube Template

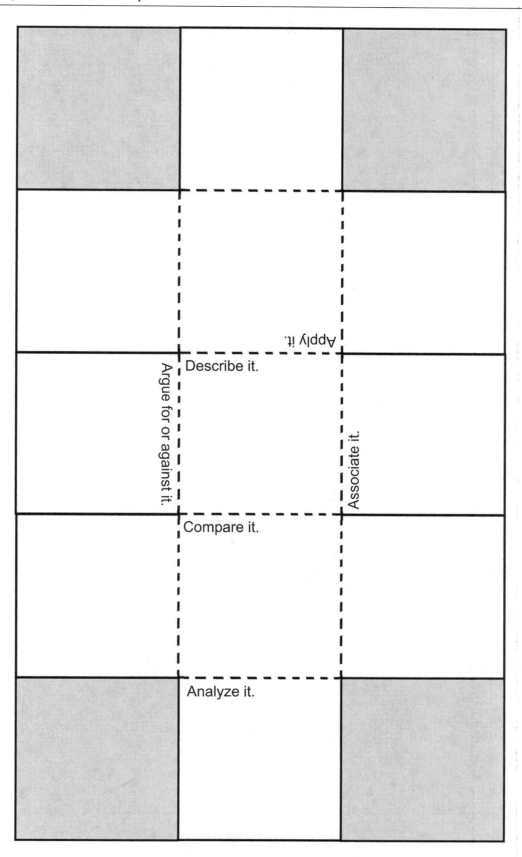

Figure 12.2   Cubing

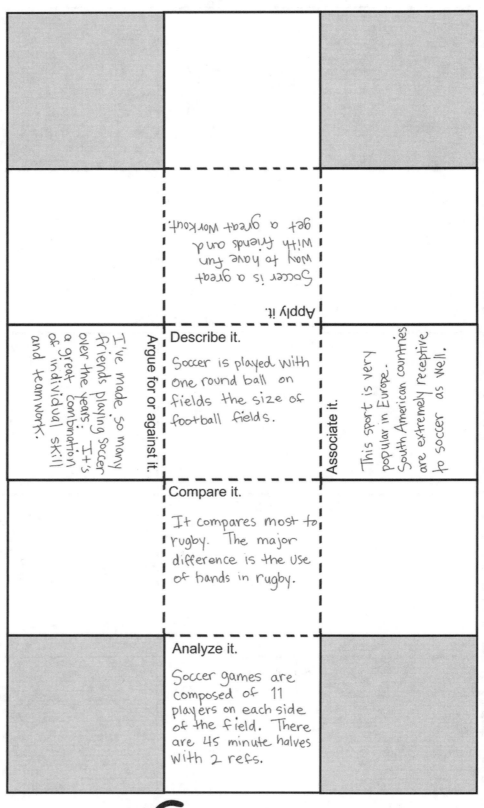

Apply it.

Soccer is a great way to have fun with friends and get a great workout.

Argue for or against it.

I've made so many friends playing soccer over the years. It's a great combination of individual skill and teamwork.

Describe it.

Soccer is played with one round ball on fields the size of football fields.

Associate it.

This sport is very popular in Europe. South American countries are extremely receptive to soccer as well.

Compare it.

It compares most to rugby. The major difference is the use of hands in rugby.

Analyze it.

Soccer games are composed of 11 players on each side of the field. There are 45 minute halves with 2 refs.

Soccer

Figure 12.3a, b, and c

(a)

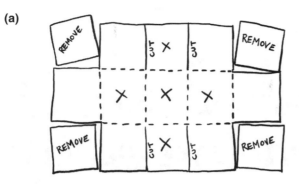

(b)

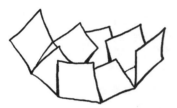

(c)

Directed Reading Thinking Activity

> Suggested Grade Levels: K to 5
>
> Elements Addressed: Plot/theme, character, expository text
>
> Meta-Strategies Incorporated: Monitoring reading for meaning (clarifying), making inferences (predicting)
>
> Supplies: Narrative or expository text, including picture books

● WHAT IS A DIRECTED READING THINKING ACTIVITY?

Directed Reading Thinking Activity, also known as DRTA, is an ongoing process in which students draw on their own experience to make predictions about the text they are reading. It was first developed in 1969 by Russell G. Stauffer to encourage readers to actively engage in a three-step comprehension process: sampling the text, making predictions, and then sampling the text again to confirm or correct previous predictions. Teachers lead DRTA discussions through active questioning. The strategy works with picture books as well as with text.

When Do We Use It?

Teachers begin this activity before students read and continue it throughout the reading process. Before reading, the teacher invites students to make predictions and thereby establishes a purpose for reading the segment. After reading, the teacher uses questions to direct the children back to their predictions for confirmation, modification, and creation of new predictions for the upcoming segment.

Two types of questions are typically asked in a DRTA. *Before* reading a segment, the teacher asks questions that require speculation and prediction (e.g., "What do you think?" "Why do you think so?" and "What makes you think that?"). *After* reading, the questions require support for conclusions (e.g., "What makes you think that?" "Why?" and "How do you know that?").

Why Do We Use It?

DRTA encourages students to think about the text and make predictions about it. Students then read or listen closely to find out if their predictions are correct.

DRTA has been adopted by most basal reading series in preference to the older and questionable round-robin format. With more than twenty-five years of changes and adjustments (e.g., Caldwell 1991), the strategy continues to be widely used, especially with young and struggling readers, because its framework enables the teacher to provide targeted, direct instruction. DRTA is highly supportive for the reader (and therefore time-intensive for the teacher).

How Do We Use the Directed Reading Thinking Activity?

Before beginning this activity, the teacher reads the text and chooses several key places where students will stop reading and make predictions about what might happen next.

Before students begin reading, the teacher introduces the book, starting by announcing the title and showing the cover. After listening to the title and viewing the cover, students respond to the teacher's questions:

- What do you think a story with a title like this might be about?
- What does the illustration on the cover tell you about what the story might be about?
- What do you think might happen in the story?
- Why do you think that?

Next, the teacher reads the first couple of paragraphs and then asks more questions:

- Now what do you think a story with a title like this might be about?
- What does the illustration on the cover tell you now about what the story might be about?
- Now what do you think might happen?
- Why do you think that now?

The teacher ends this questioning period by asking,

- Did you change your prediction? If so, why?

Students begin reading and continue until they have reached a designated page. At the stopping point, students respond to the following questions:

- What do you think now?
- What do you think will happen next?
- Why do you think that?
- How do you know that?
- Did you change your prediction? If so, why?

The process continues, with stops for discussion at several key points.

After students have finished reading the entire book, they reflect on their predictions. The teacher encourages students to think about the story, to make personal connections, and to express their feelings about the story. The teacher might also ask the following:

- What predictions did you make?
- Were you correct?
- Why did you think that?
- How do you know?
- How did your predictions compare to what really happened?

How Else Can We Use This Strategy?

Directed Listening Thinking Activity (DLTA): DLTA is an adaptation of Stauffer's (1975) DRTA. During DLTA, emergent readers listen to a story read aloud, predict, and continue to listen to confirm or correct their predictions. DLTA has become popular for helping emergent readers develop a sense of story.

Picture Walk: For young students listening to a picture book, the teacher begins by showing the cover and reading the title. Next, as a group, students view the pictures in the book, looking at each picture and predicting what they think is happening in the story. Afterward, students listen to the story and then discuss whether their predictions were correct and what really happened.

Guided Reading Groups: The DRTA strategy is commonly used with small reading groups while other groups are engaged in follow-up activities such as writing or independent reading. Working with the guided reading group, the teacher elicits predictions, asks students to read the segment, encourages students to discuss their predictions in light of their reading, and asks each student to reread orally relevant sentences or paragraphs to clarify answers.

Where Can We Learn More?

Caldwell, J. (1991). A new look at the old guided reading lesson. *Wisconsin State Reading Association Journal, 35*(2), 1–7.

Headley, K. N., & Dunston, P. J. (2000). Teachers' choices books and comprehension strategies as transaction tools. *The Reading Teacher, 54,* 260–268.

Morrow, L. M. (1984). Reading stories to young children: Effects of story structure and traditional questioning strategies on comprehension. *Journal of Reading Behavior, 16,* 273–288.

Richek, M. A. (1987). DRTA: Five variations that facilitate independence in reading narratives. *Journal of Reading, 30,* 632–636.

Stauffer, R. G. (1969). *Directing reading maturity as a cognitive process.* New York: HarperCollins.

Stauffer, R. G. (1975). *Directing the reading-thinking process.* New York: Harper & Row.

Tompkins, G. E. (2004). *Fifty literacy strategies: Step by step* (2nd ed.). Upper Saddle River, NJ: Pearson-Prentice Hall.

Figure 13.1

Directed Reading Thinking Activity

Based on *First Day Jitters*

Predictions made before the story:

- The little girl does not want to go to school.
- Her cat and dog are her friends.
- She is scared of something.
- She doesn't feel good.

Predictions made through the story:

- Her dad is getting mad at her.
- Her dog and cat are mad at each other.
- Her dad doesn't know how to get her out of bed.
- The girl is going to hide so she doesn't have to go to school.
- She is going to run out of the car.
- Her class is going to be nice to her.

Reflections on predictions after reading:

- I can't believe that she was really the teacher.
- Teachers get nervous too, I guess.
- She was being silly.
- That was not her dad; it was her husband.
- She had a nice husband.
- Her class was nice to her.

Book used: Danneberg, J. (2000). *First day jitters.* Watertown, MA: Charlesbridge.

Contributed by Brooke Nylen, San Francisco, CA, Fall 2003.

14

Double-Entry Journal

Also Called: Dialectical Journal

Suggested Grade Levels: 3 to 8

Elements Addressed: Plot/theme, character, expository text

Meta-Strategies Incorporated: Making connections

Supplies: Narrative or expository text, lined paper, pens or pencils

● WHAT IS A DOUBLE-ENTRY JOURNAL?

A double-entry journal is a response journal divided into two parts. In the left column, students write quotations from the text; in the right, they respond to and ask questions about those quotations.

When Do We Use It?

A double-entry journal is a good tool to use during or after reading a book. It can be used to get students thinking before a discussion.

Why Do We Use It?

Use of this strategy improves comprehension of text. It encourages students to make meaning of and interact with what they read. While working with their double-entry journals, students read critically and build personal connections to what they read. They explore ideas, reading thoughtfully and not just literally, and are encouraged to ask questions. Typically, they relate the quotations to their own lives and to other books they have read.

The strategy also helps students build writing skills. It gets them to explore ideas and take risks in their writing.

How Do We Use Double-Entry Journals?

Students divide a sheet of paper into two columns. They label the left-hand column "Quotes" or "Text" and the right-hand column "Comments," "Reflections," or "Response." As they read, or immediately after they read, they select some interesting and/or important quotations from the text and write them in the left-hand column. The teacher may want to tell students how many quotes to select.

After students have selected their quotes, they write their responses to those selections in the right-hand column. Students may relate the quote to something in their own lives, or they may write about their reaction to it. They may also make drawings or other illustrations to respond to quotes (especially if they are in the younger grades). In any case, students make some sort of personal connection to the literature.

Students may also write reflective questions in the right-hand column. Composing such questions requires the student to think carefully about the quotation. These questions may be used to initiate a longer writing assignment or to begin a class discussion.

How Else Can We Use This Strategy?

Teacher Quotations: The teacher chooses quotations for students to write in the left-hand column. Students respond as they like or write questions about the quotation before discussing it as a group.

Dialectical Notebook: After writing quotations and responses in a notebook, students pass their journals to other students for responses.

Dialogue Journals: Students react to their reading or another topic in a journal. The teacher then collects the journals, responds to them in writing, and returns them to the students. See also Learning Logs.

Where Can We Learn More?

Barone, D. (1990). The written responses of young children: Beyond comprehension to story understanding. *The New Advocate, 3,* 49–56.

Bromley, K. (1993). Journaling: Engagements in reading, writing, and thinking. *Teaching Strategies.* New York: Scholastic.

Fulwiler, T. (Ed.). (1987). *The journal book.* Portsmouth, NH: Boynton/Cook, Heinemann.

Macon, J. M., Bewell, D., & Vogt, M. E. (1991). *Responses to literature: Grades K–8.* Newark, DE: International Reading Association.

McLaughlin, M., & Allen, M. B. (2002). *Guided Comprehension: A teaching model for grades 3–8.* Newark: International Reading Association.

Schulz, A. R. (1998). *Supporting intermediate and secondary readers: Selected interactive approaches.* Costa Mesa, CA: California Reading Association.

Figure 14.1

Double-Entry Journal

Based on the Novel *The Slave Dancer*

Text	Response
Chapter 2: "The Moonlight"	
I thought desperately of my mother and Betty in the room with apricot brocade. I cursed the rich stuff and the lady who had ordered a gown from my mother, and the candles I had gotten from Aunt Agatha. I cursed myself for taking the longest way home. (p. 15)	When I find myself in a situation I don't want to be in, I sometimes backtrack to see how I got into the mess. I don't necessarily curse the possible causes, but I do play around with the causes to see how the situation might have turned out differently.
For all the calmness with which he said *Africa*, he might as well have said Royal Street. I felt like a bird caught in a room. (p. 18)	I can visualize a bird frantically flying around a room bumping into the walls. The need to fly free is so great that the bird doesn't realize it's hurting itself.
The first object my eyes rested upon was crawling idly along my leg as though I was a yard of bread. The insect was no stranger to me for we had them in all sizes at home. But I'd never thought a cockroach was a seagoing creature. I didn't care for the breed. Still, I found it a touch comforting that such a familiar land thing was making itself at home on me. (p. 23)	Jesse must really miss home. Of course he does, but when a cockroach starts providing comfort even if only a touch, life is not good.

I like how there is a buildup to the introduction of the cockroach. It further pronounces Jesse's miserable situation. |

Book used: Fox, P. (1973). *The slave dancer*. New York: Bantam Doubleday Dell Books for Young Readers.

Contributed by China Byon, San Francisco, CA, Fall 2003.

15

Exclusion Brainstorming

Suggested Grade Levels: 3 to 8

Elements Addressed: Plot/theme, character, expository text

Meta-Strategies Incorporated: Asking questions, making inferences (predicting)

Supplies: Text with social studies or science subject matter, a board or flipchart, dark-colored markers

WHAT IS EXCLUSION BRAINSTORMING? •

Exclusion brainstorming is a strategy in which students use their prior knowledge to anticipate new concepts. It involves thinking about words and determining whether or not they relate to a given topic. It works with fiction or nonfiction text, especially with social studies or science subject matter.

When Do We Use It?

Students begin this strategy before they read. They continue during reading.

Why Do We Use It?

Exclusion brainstorming forces students to think about what they know about a topic before they begin reading. At the same time, they begin to work with vocabulary related to the upcoming reading. The activity also gives students a reason for reading as they search for the selected words.

How Do We Use Exclusion Brainstorming?

Before students begin reading a story or text, the teacher develops a list of words, some related to the upcoming reading and others not. The teacher writes the words on the board or flipchart with the title or topic of the selection at the top. Beneath the title or topic, the teacher writes some words that come from the story and fit the topic, some words that clearly do not fit the topic, and a few words that are ambiguous.

Students begin by reading through the words and deciding which words they think will *not* be found in the selection. A group recorder underlines those words. Students then determine which words they think *are* related to the text subject. The recorder circles those words. Students should be able to explain, either orally or in writing, why they think the way they do.

During discussion, the teacher calls attention to important words and concepts for the upcoming reading. Through this strategy, teachers are able to blend schema activation and vocabulary analysis and to directly link both to the reading selection.

As students read, they watch for the words or concepts, checking off words that appear. After they have finished, they cross out any words that do not relate.

How Else Can We Use This Strategy?

Independent Work: Instead of writing words on a board or flipchart, the teacher distributes a handout with the words listed and students make their own selections as to which words are related and which are not.

Where Can We Learn More?

Blachowicz, C. L. Z. (1986). Making connections: Alternatives to the vocabulary notebook. *Journal of Reading, 29*(7), 643–649.

Tompkins, G. E. (2004). *Fifty literacy strategies: Step by step* (2nd ed.). Upper Saddle River, NJ: Pearson-Prentice Hall.

Figure 15.1   Exclusion Brainstorming

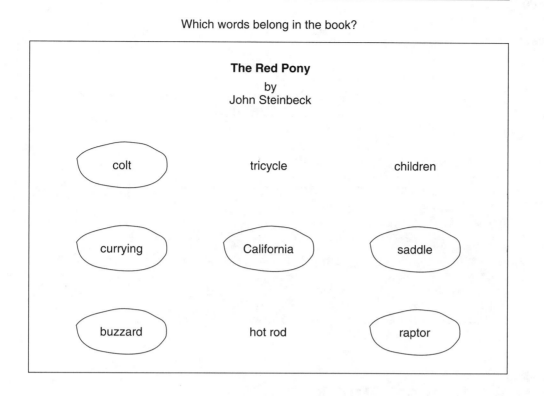

Which words belong in the book?

The Red Pony
by
John Steinbeck

colt   tricycle   children

currying   California   saddle

buzzard   hot rod   raptor

16

Fishbowl

Suggested Grade Levels: 6 to 8

Elements Addressed: Plot/theme, character, expository text

Meta-Strategies Incorporated: Making connections, asking questions

Supplies: Narrative or expository text, one chair for each student, student-prepared questions about the text

● WHAT IS A FISHBOWL?

A fishbowl is an arrangement of students with the purpose of discussing literature. Participants sitting in an inner circle actively discuss the literature; they ask questions they have prepared, answer other students' questions, and debate issues. Students in an outer circle watch, listen, and evaluate the process.

When Do We Use It?

This strategy is used after students have completed their reading and developed some questions based on it.

Why Do We Use It?

The fishbowl strategy develops classroom community and promotes participation. Students analyze the text, develop their own questions, and together clarify controversial aspects of the text. Other students listen actively and evaluate their classmates' discussion.

How Do We Use the Fishbowl Strategy?

Before beginning this activity, students are instructed to develop a list of questions based on a completed reading. Each student may write three or four questions.

Chairs are placed in two circles, one within the other. The inner circle, or fishbowl, has seven chairs in it; the outer circle has enough chairs to seat the rest of the class. Five students are selected to be panelists, and they take their place in five of the inner-circle chairs, leaving empty two inner-circle chairs placed opposite each other. These two chairs are "jump seats," to be used by students who wish to jump into the discussion and then return to the audience.

Students in the inner circle take turns asking questions, giving answers, and discussing. Other students listen, jumping in as they like and as a jump seat becomes available. The students in the inner circle, or fishbowl, summarize their discussion at the end of the period.

Fishbowl

Any student in the outer circle may jump into one of the two "jump seats" at any time to be interviewed by the panel. Only those students sitting INSIDE the fishbowl may speak. All others must actively listen and observe.

How Else Can We Use This Strategy?

Intense Discussion: A third jump seat is added for intense discussions.

Where Can We Learn More?

Baron, Leora (2004). *"Fishbowl" Discussion.* Teaching and Learning Center, University of Nevada, Las Vegas. Retrieved June 10, 2005 from http://tlc.unlv.edu/articles/ClassroomManagement/tlc_fishbowldiscussion.pdf

Fountas, I. C., & Pinnel, G. S. (2001). *Guiding readers and writers, grades 3–6.* Portsmouth, NH: Heinemann.

Lindenberg, G. (2001). *Fishbowl Discussion of* The American. ExxonMobil Masterpiece Theatre's American Collection Educators Site. Retrieved June 10, 2005 from http://www.ncteamericancollection.org/amer_fishbowl_lessonplan.htm

Lubliner, S. (2001). Fishbowl. In S. Lubliner (Ed.), *A practical guide to reciprocal teaching* (pp. 59–62, 145). Bothell, WA: Wright Group/McGraw-Hill.

Priles, M. A. (1993). The fishbowl discussion: A strategy for larger honors classes. *English Journal, 82*(6), 49–50.

17

Found Poem

Suggested Grade Levels: 3 to 8

Elements Addressed: Plot/theme, character, expository text

Meta-Strategies Incorporated: Monitoring reading for meaning (clarifying), determining important information

Supplies: Narrative or expository text, strips of paper, lined paper, pencils or crayons

WHAT IS A FOUND POEM? ●

A found poem is a poem created from meaningful words or phrases chosen by students from a piece of literature. The found poem conveys the meaning of the literature.

When Do We Use It?

This strategy can be used after students have read individual chapters or the entire book.

Why Do We Use It?

The strategy forces students to focus on the author's words and how those words convey the meaning of the story. Students become aware of descriptive writing. They also learn to interpret the author's words in their own way.

How Do We Use Found Poems?

The teacher begins this activity with a discussion of rationale for organizing ideas in a "poem". The class works together to create a first found poem. Then, after initial modeling, students may work individually, in pairs, or in small groups.

To create a found poem, students first choose words and phrases that are significant to them and capture the meaning of a story. They copy the words or phrases onto strips of paper, with one set of words on each strip. Then they arrange the words and phrases to create poetry. Depending on the students' ages, they may use such poetic devices as repeated refrains, patterned question and response, sound effects, parallel construction of phrases, and/or stream of consciousness.

After students have created their work, they copy the poem onto a single sheet of paper. They may also wish to illustrate their poem. Students then have the opportunity to share their poem with the larger group.

How Else Can We Use This Strategy?

Character Found Poem: Students use only quotes about or from a particular character.

Where Can We Learn More?

Claggett, F., Reid, L., & Vinz, R. (1996). *Recasting the Text.* Portsmouth, NH: Boynton/Cook Heinemann.

Commeyras, M., & Karly, K. (2002). A "found" poem from a reading odyssey. *Journal of Adolescent and Adult Literacy, 46*(2), 100–102.

Dunning, S., & Stafford, W. (1992). Found and headline poems. *Getting the Knack: Twenty Poetry Writing Exercises.* Urbana, IL: National Council of Teachers of English.

Gorrell, N. (1989). Let found poetry help your students find poetry. *English Journal, 78*(2), 30–34.

Hester, P. O. (1989). The found poem. *Reading Teacher, 42*(4), 342.

Phillips, D. (1989). Let found poetry help your students study literature. *English Journal, 78*(5), 68–70.

Figure 17.1

Found Poem

Based on the Novel *The Planet of Junior Brown*

Buddy

Homeless and Alone

Dark in a Basement

Secret Hideout

Piano

Insane

Planet of Junior Brown

Book used: Hamilton, V. (1971). *The planet of Junior Brown.* New York: Simon & Schuster Children's Publishing.

Contributed by Brooke Sibley, San Francisco, CA, Fall 2003.

Figure 17.2   Sample found poem based on *Friends from the Other Side*

Found Poem

Based on *Friends from the Other Side*

Mexican - US border

Many have crossed because there is work

Look at the "mojadito"

Stop!

Friends

He returned the next day and the next

Border Patrol

They'll take her away!

A place to hide

A new friend

I will teach you

You are ready now

Book used: Anzaldua, G. (1995). Friends from the Other Side/Amigos del otro lado. San Francisco, CA: Children's Book Press.

Contributed by Kristina Reguero and Lindsay Kahn, San Francisco, CA, Summer 2004.

18

Four-Corners Debate

Suggested Grade Levels: 6 to 8

Elements Addressed: Plot/theme, expository text

Meta-Strategies Incorporated: Summarizing and synthesizing

Supplies: Any text with controversial or debatable subject matter, four large sheets of drawing paper, board or flipchart, dark-colored markers

● WHAT IS A FOUR-CORNERS DEBATE?

A four-corners debate is a discussion among students with different opinions about a complex issue presented within a text. It involves the entire class and forces students to form and support their opinions about the chosen issue. Students should be able to support their opinions with evidence from the text.

When Do We Use It?

This strategy may be used at any time an issue in a reading provokes conversation and stirs up different opinions.

Why Do We Use It?

The four-corners debate forces students to reflect on their reading, to express their thoughts about a topic, and to use reason to draw conclusions. It also provides a forum for students to interact, listen to the perspectives of others, and perhaps change their opinions based on what they hear.

How Do We Use the Four-Corners Debate?

The teacher begins by making four signs with the following words on them: "Agree," "Disagree," "Strongly Agree," and "Strongly Disagree." One sign is then placed in each corner of the room. Next, a statement is written on the board to provoke student opinion or reaction.

Students move to the corner of the room with the sign that expresses their opinion: agree, disagree, strongly agree, or strongly disagree. They then discuss their reactions to the statement with other students who share their opinion. The teacher lets them know when they have only five minutes left to discuss. Each group selects a leader to share the group's opinions.

The groups take turns sharing their opinions with the other groups. After each group has had a turn, the floor is opened for student debate. Students may change corners if they change their opinion but must explain why they changed.

Where Can We Learn More?

Hopkins, G. (2003). *Four corner debate.* Retrieved March 3, 2005, from http://www .education-world.com/a_lesson/03/lp304–04.shtml

Kagan, S. (1989). Corners. *The Structural Approach to Cooperative Learning. Educational Leadership, 47* (December/January), 8–12.

Leonard, J. (1999). *From monologue to dialogue: Facilitating classroom debate.* Paper presented at the Joint Annual Meeting of the School Science and Mathematics Association and the North Carolina Council of Teachers of Mathematics, October.

Worthen, T. K., & Pack, G. N. (1992). *Classroom debate as an experiential activity across the curriculum.* Paper presented at the Seventy-eighth Annual Meeting of the Speech Communication Association, Chicago, October 29 to November 1.

19

Gallery Walk

Suggested Grade Levels: K to 8

Elements Addressed: Plot/theme, character, expository text

Meta-Strategies Incorporated: Making connections, asking questions, summarizing and synthesizing

Supplies: Narrative or expository text, butcher paper, lined paper, pens or pencils, tape

 ## WHAT IS A GALLERY WALK?

A gallery walk is an exhibit of students' comments about, questions about, and personal responses to a reading selection. Students walk through the gallery to view each other's thoughts just as one might walk through an art gallery to view artwork.

When Do We Use It?

Students write down and exhibit their thoughts after completing their reading.

Why Do We Use It?

This strategy allows students to exhibit their thoughts about a piece of writing. It also allows students to see what their peers have written about the same piece of writing and to compare their thoughts.

How Do We Use the Gallery Walk?

The teacher hangs three large pieces of butcher paper in the room. At the top of one is the label "Comments." Another is labeled "Questions." The third is titled "Personal Responses."

After students have completed their reading, they are instructed to write down their thoughts for each of the three categories listed on the butcher paper. They then cut out their writing and tape the three thoughts to the corresponding butcher paper.

After all students have displayed their thoughts, they walk around the "gallery" to see what others have written. Finally, students take their seats and discuss what they have seen. They may ask for clarification of comments, suggest answers to questions, or build on or question responses.

How Else Can We Use This Strategy?

Facts/Questions/Responses: Instead of comments, students may record facts they have learned from a nonfiction piece of writing.

Where Can We Learn More?

Smart, M., & Calcutt, L. (1999). Power walking on the broadwater. *Practically Primary, 4*(3), 29–32.

Figure 19.1

Gallery Walk Exhibit

Based on the Novel *The Giver*

Comments

Jonas is chosen as the new Giver for the Community.

The Giver gets to "experience" the things others in the Community do not. The Giver experiences for the others.

People are assigned roles in the Community.

Questions

How will Jonas and Gabriel handle life outside the Community where there will be so much choice?

What role would I be given if I was a member of the Community?

How did Jonas's family feel when they discovered he was gone?

Personal Responses

Not having pain and sadness seems tempting, but the Community is so bleak.

Perfection comes at too high a cost.

The "experiences" of the Giver allow him to truly give.

Book used: Lowry, L. (1993). *The giver.* New York: Dell Laurel-Leaf.

Contributed by China Byon, San Francisco, CA, Fall 2003.

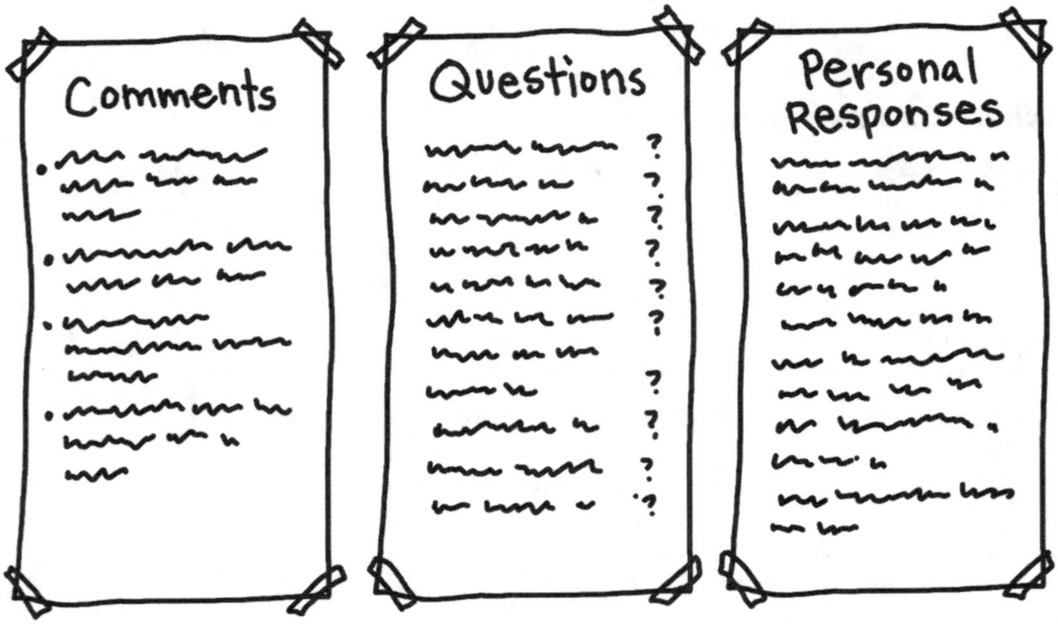
Comments
Questions
Personal Responses

Grand Conversation

Suggested Grade Levels: K to 8

Elements Addressed: Plot/theme, character, expository text

Meta-Strategies Incorporated: Making connections, summarizing and synthesizing

Supplies: Narrative or expository text, lined paper and pencils for each person to jot notes (optional), chairs for participants placed in a circle

WHAT IS A GRAND CONVERSATION?

A grand conversation is a group discussion of a text read by all participants. A group leader, usually the teacher, encourages students to think about what they have read, make interpretations, and share their thoughts. The teacher may facilitate, but the discussion takes place primarily among students.

When Do We Use It?

A grand conversation is effective after students have read a section or chapter of a book or after they have completed the entire book.

Why Do We Use It?

The grand conversation encourages students to consider a text carefully and to interpret what they have read. It also encourages students to listen and respond to what other students think about the text. In so doing, students expand on their own ideas and make connections.

How Do We Use the Grand Conversation?

Students read a section of a book or, if young, listen as the teacher reads aloud. They then sit in a circle so that they can see each other. The teacher suggests a topic for discussion, perhaps simply, "What did this story mean to you?" The focus may be on illustrations, the author, or literary elements, or students may compare the book to another book or to a movie made from the book.

Serving as group leader, or facilitator, the teacher keeps the conversation going and even joins in occasionally but allows students to do most of the talking. Each student must participate, either by making a comment, building on the comment of a classmate, or asking a question. The facilitator limits each student to one or two comments until everyone has spoken at least once. Students may refer back to the book, read a short bit of text (but not a long passage), or read from their own writing. The facilitator also makes sure that students have time to reflect and comment on topics before shifting to a new topic. The teacher or facilitator keeps notes on topics and issues that emerge and uses the notes to encourage discussion. When grand conversation time is almost over, the teacher summarizes patterns that emerged and insights that have been gained.

How Else Can We Use This Strategy?

Student Leader: A student volunteer—rather than the teacher—serves as facilitator.

Journal Writing: Students jot down their thoughts about the literature before the conversation begins. They may also write their thoughts after the conversation ends.

Literature Study Groups: Instead of discussing the book or section as an entire class, students discuss in small groups. After these group discussions, the whole group comes together to discuss.

Pattern Report: One student keeps a record of topics and issues discussed. At the end of the discussion, the student reviews the record and notes any patterns that have emerged.

Video Comparison: Through a grand conversation, students compare and contrast a book to a video version of the same book.

Where Can We Learn More?

Eeds, M., & Wells, D. (1989). Grand conversations: An exploration of meaning construction in literature study groups. *Research in the Teaching of English, 22,* 4–29.

Gambell, L. B., & Almasi, J. F. (Eds.). (1996). *Lively discussions! Fostering engaged reading.* Newark, DE: International Reading Association.

McCutchen, D. (1993). Literature study groups with at-risk readers: Extending the grand conversation. *Reading Horizons, 33*(4), 313–328.

Moss, J. F. (2002). *Literary discussion in the elementary school.* Urbana, IL: National Council of Teachers of English.

Peterson, R., & Eeds, M. (1990). *Grand conversations: Literature groups in action.* New York: Scholastic.

Serafini, F. (2000). Before the conversations become "grand." *The California Reader, 33*(3), 19–24.

Spiegel, D. L. (1998). Silver bullets, babies, and bath water: Literature response groups in a balanced literacy program. *The Reading Teacher, 52,* 114–124.

Figure 20.1

Tips for the Teacher

In orchestrating a successful Grand Conversation, keep the following guidelines in mind:

- Know your students. This will help determine what kinds of questions are most likely to be productive for them and which questions draw on a particular student's experiences.
- Listen carefully to what each student is saying. Try to comprehend what is being said. Try to formulate responses that accurately reflect students' ideas.
- Try to respond to a student's idea in a way that calls for the examination of that idea from a fresh perspective.
- Choose a follow-up response that takes the student's thinking one step further.
- Decide when the interactive dialogue with that student is "finished," and when it is time to move to another student.
- Frame questions and responses so that they are always respectful, nonthreatening, and productive.
- Know the "right" time to challenge a student's thinking.
- Know which kinds of questions are more effective with which students.
- Know when to shift gears into the territory of the next big idea.
- Refrain from responding evaluatively to the students' ideas. Avoid such statements as "Good idea" and even "That's interesting." Try instead to accept students' ideas nonjudgmentally, with responses such as "I see" or "Thank you." Ask for more analysis of the idea: "Can you give me an example?" "Why do you suppose that was good?" and "How does that compare with this?"
- Do not look for single, correct answers.
- Do not talk too much or explain things your way.
- Work the interactive dialogue so that meanings are searched for, understanding grows, student thinking about the issues occurs, and students feel safe in telling what they think.

..ided Imagery

Also Called: Visual Representation

Suggested Grade Levels: K to 8

Elements Addressed: Plot/theme, character

Meta-Strategies Incorporated: Visualizing

Supplies: Text with descriptive language, newspaper or a book cover, drawing paper, crayons or markers

---

● WHAT IS GUIDED IMAGERY?

Guided imagery is a strategy through which students form original mental images of the setting or characters in a piece of literature read aloud to them. They choose one image and draw it on paper.

When Do We Use It?

This strategy is used as a book is read aloud and continued after the reading ends.

Why Do We Use It?

Students use their imaginations to interpret a story. As they see the characters and settings in their minds, they develop clear comprehension of the story. After forming their own artistic interpretations, they are able to verbalize their ideas.

How Do We Use Guided Imagery?

The teacher chooses a book with lots of vivid, descriptive language. Any illustrations on the cover or jacket are hidden from the students with a book cover or newspaper. The teacher tells the students to shut their eyes and listen as the book is read aloud. Students are instructed to make their own illustrations in their minds as the book is read.

After the teacher has finished reading, students are asked to choose the most vivid picture they formed in their mind and draw it on paper. Afterward, the teacher rereads the book, this time showing the original illustrations. Students are invited to share their drawings at the appropriate time.

Figure 21.1

Guided Imagery

For Primary Students
Based on the Book *Snow*

Read aloud to students in Grades K to 2 the book *Snow*, by Uri Shulevitz. Do not show children the pictures as you read. Ask children to close their eyes and make pictures in their minds.

Ask the children to pick one scene from the book and draw a picture of it as they saw it "in their heads." Remind them that everyone will have a slightly different interpretation of how the characters and setting looked.

After children have shared and discussed their drawings, reread the book, this time showing the illustrations.

Book used: Shulevitz, U. (1998). *Snow.* New York: Farrar, Strauss.

Illustration contributed by Brooke Sibley, San Francisco, CA, Fall 2003.

Contributed by Brooke Sibley, San Francisco, CA, Fall 2003.

See also Figure 40.2: Quickwrite with Guided Imagery for older students.

How Else Can We Use This Strategy?

Compare and Contrast: Students may compare and contrast their pictures with those in the book.

Word Text: For a book without many pictures, students may read to themselves, visualizing as they read, and then draw one image on paper.

Where Can We Learn More?

Armstrong, T. (2003). *The multiple intelligences of reading and writing.* Alexandria, VA: Association for Supervision and Curriculum Development.

Gambrell, L. B., & Koskinen, P. S. (2002). Imagery: A strategy for enhancing comprehension. In C. C. Block & M. Presley (Eds.), *Comprehension instruction: Research-based practices* (pp. 305–318). New York: Guilford.

Harvey, S., & Goudvis, A. (2000). Visualizing and inferring: Strategies that enhance understanding. In S. Harvey, A. Goudvis, & P. Stratton (Eds.), *Strategies that work: Teaching comprehension to enhance understanding* (pp. 95–116, 274–281). Portland, ME: Stenhouse.

Hibbing, A., & Rankin-Erickson, J. L. (2003). A picture is worth a thousand words: Using visual images to improve comprehension for middle school readers. *The Reading Teacher, 56,* 758–770.

Keene, E. O., & Zimmerman, S. (1997). A mosaic in the mind: Using sensory images to enhance comprehension. In E. O. Keene (Ed.), *Mosaic of thought: Teaching comprehension in a reader's workshop* (pp. 123–143). Portsmouth, NH: Heinemann.

Wilhelm, J. (2004). *Reading IS seeing: Learning to visualize scenes, characters, ideas, and text world, to improve comprehension and reflective reading.* New York: Scholastic.

22

Hot Seat

Suggested Grade Levels: K to 8

Elements Addressed: Character

Meta-Strategies Incorporated: Asking questions, making inferences, summarizing and synthesizing

Supplies: Any fiction or nonfiction text with strong characters in it, masks or props representative of the chosen characters (optional)

WHAT IS A HOT SEAT? ●

The hot seat is a chair used by a student who has assumed the personality of a character in the literature. Other students ask questions of the student in the hot seat, and that student answers the questions from the selected character's perspective.

When Do We Use It?

This strategy works well at the end of a chapter or after students have finished reading the entire book.

Why Do We Use It?

The student in the hot seat thinks about questions from the point of view of one character in the story. The student must think about how that character might respond to questions and thereby gains understanding of the character. Students who are not in the hot seat learn to ask meaningful, open-ended questions. Through the strategy, students gain perspective of the attitudes and views of different characters.

How Do We Use the Hot Seat Strategy?

The teacher introduces this strategy by modeling it, choosing a character to represent from a piece of literature recently read. The teacher sits in a chair designated as the hot seat. A puppet or a character mask may be used to represent the character, or the teacher may wear an article of clothing, such as a hat or tie, typical of that character. The teacher then tells the students to think of questions they might ask of that character; students should avoid questions that can be answered with a simple "yes" or "no." Volunteers are called on to ask their questions, and the teacher answers in the voice of the character, also explaining why the represented character might answer in that way.

Next, a student volunteers to act as one of the characters in the book. This student sits in the hot seat, using a puppet, a character mask, or an article of clothing to represent the character. Classmates ask questions of the student in the hot seat, and that student answers the questions as he or she thinks the represented character would answer them.

After a predetermined amount of time—perhaps two minutes—the student steps out of the hot seat and another student takes a place, perhaps portraying the same character or perhaps portraying another. Alternatively, the teacher may set a limit on number of questions—perhaps three or four questions for each student in the hot seat.

How Else Can We Use This Strategy?

Brainstorming Questions: Before a student takes the hot seat, other students work in small groups to brainstorm possible questions for the given character. After a certain amount of time, they ask their questions of the person in the hot seat.

Historical Character: If the text is nonfiction, the teacher may select a historical event on which to focus.

Small Groups: Students work in groups of three to five, with each student choosing one character to represent. One student sits in the hot seat, while the others ask questions of that character. After two minutes, another student takes a turn in the hot seat representing a different character.

Multiple Characters: The students who are asking questions take on the personalities of other characters from the book.

Multiple Hot Seats: Different students take on the personalities of different characters and sit together at the front of the classroom for questioning.

Where Can We Learn More?

Lubliner, S. (2001). Hot seat. In S. Lubilner (Ed.), *A practical guide to reciprocal teaching* (pp. 27–31). Bothell, WA: Wright Group/McGraw-Hill.

Tompkins, G. E. (2004). *Fifty literacy strategies: Step by step* (2nd ed.). Upper Saddle River, NJ: Prentice Hall.

Van Horn, L. (1997). The characters within us: Readers connect with characters to create meaning and understanding. *Journal of Adolescent and Adult Literacy, 40,* 342–347.

Wilhelm, J. (2002). *Action strategies for deepening comprehension.* New York: Scholastic.

Wilson, G. P. (2003). Supporting young children's thinking through tableau. *Language Arts, 80*(5): 375–383.

Figure 22.1

Hot Seat

Planning Sheet

Name _____   Date _____

1. Book Title _____

2. Author _____

3. Character _____

4. Character Traits _____

   _____

   _____

1) Questions to ask the Hot Seat person:

   a) _____

   _____

   b) _____

   _____

   c) _____

Copyright © 2006 by Corwin Press. All rights reserved. Reprinted from *60 Strategies for Improving Reading Comprehension in Grades K – 8*, by Kathleen Feeney Jonson. Thousand Oaks, CA: Corwin Press, www.corwinpress.com. Reproduction authorized only for the local school site that has purchased this book.

Figure 22.2

HOT SEAT

Based on the Novel *Holes*

A sixth-grade class is reading *Holes,* by Louis Sachar. At the end of each chapter, the class participates in a Hot Seat activity, using one or several characters from the book, depending on who was most relevant in that chapter. For this Hot Seat activity, one student represents the main character, Stanley Yelnats. The class is asking Stanley open-ended questions.

Audience: How did you feel when you were falsely accused of stealing the shoes?

Stanley: I was hurt and upset. I didn't understand why no one believed me. I am a good kid. I was at the wrong place at the wrong time.

Audience: Did you always believe in the story about your no-good-dirty-rotten-pig-stealing great great grandfather?

Stanley: Yes. I had no reason not to believe it. Bad things always happened to the men in my family. It just made sense.

Audience: What was your dad's greatest invention?

Stanley: Definitely his cure for foot odor. I got to meet Clyde Livingston and become his friend. Clyde is even the spokesman for it now!

Audience: What was your least favorite part about Camp Greenlake?

Stanley: I hated all of it! Except for the friends I made, of course. If I had to pick one thing, I think it would be the yellow-spotted lizards. Yeck!

Book used: Sachar, L. (1998). *Holes.* New York: Frances Foster Books.

Contributed by Kate Working, San Francisco, CA, Fall 2003.

Figure 22.3

Hot Seat

Based on the Story *The Mitten*

A first grade class has listened to a read-aloud of *The Mitten.* The Hot Seat student has chosen to be the boy, Nickie.

Audience Question #1: Why did you want snow white mittens?

Answer: I wanted white mittens because white is the color of snow.

Audience Question #2: When you noticed your mitten was missing, how did you feel?

Answer: I felt sad because my grandmother had made it for me.

Audience Question #3: How did you feel when you caught your mitten?

Answer: I felt happy because I'd found my mitten.

(Note: For primary children, limit the number of questions to three and then choose another student for the Hot Seat. Before using this strategy, discuss and give examples of how to ask good questions, answer in complete sentences, avoid "yes" and "no" answers, and show how the character in the story feels.)

Book used: Brett, J. (1996). *The Mitten: A Ukrainian Folktale.* New York: Putnam.

Contributed by Christine Labagh, San Francisco, CA, Summer 2004.

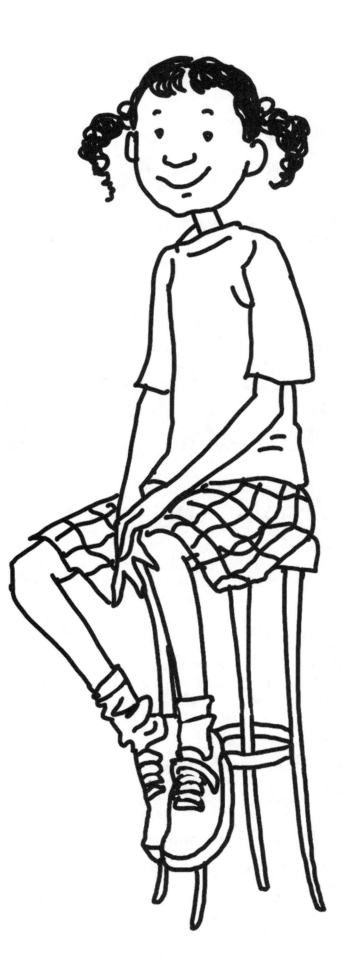

23

Interior Monologue

Suggested Grade Levels: 6 to 8

Elements Addressed: Character

Meta-Strategies Incorporated: Making inferences, summarizing and synthesizing

Supplies: Narrative text, lined paper, pens or pencils

● WHAT IS AN INTERIOR MONOLOGUE?

An interior monologue is a piece of writing in which the student takes on the personality of a character and explores that character's thoughts and feelings. Students write an interior monologue in the first person, as if they were the character.

When Do We Use It?

Students write an interior monologue after they have a full understanding of a character. This may be after they have read the entire book, or it may be sooner.

Why Do We Use It?

To write an interior monologue, students must understand a character within the story. The strategy also gives students a new writing style using stream of consciousness.

How Do We Use Interior Monologues?

Before introducing this strategy, the teacher writes an interior monologue from the perspective of one character from a piece of literature recently read by the class. The teacher then begins by telling students that they will choose a character, think about that character, and try to imagine how the character would think or feel about a particular topic. The teacher reads from the interior monologue written from the viewpoint of one character, explaining the thoughts and feelings of that character about a particular topic.

Next, students are told to choose their own character and think about the character. Finally, they have time to record the thoughts and feelings of the character in writing. They are told that writing is to be spontaneous and subjective.

Figure 23.1

Interior Monologue

Based on *Anne Frank: The Diary of a Young Girl*

Margot is driving me crazy today. Everyone is driving me crazy! I want to scream and shout, but can't even whisper. Mother tells me to have patience and trust, but I don't have anything; I feel empty. Everyday I wake up and hope that this is the day we can come out from behind the bookshelf, but it never is.

Book used: Frank, A. (1993). *Anne Frank: The diary of a young girl.* Translated by B. M. Mooyaart, with an introduction by Eleanor Roosevelt. New York: Bantam.

Contributed by Stephanie Abramowitz, San Francisco, CA, Fall 2003.

Figure 23.2

Interior Monologue

Based on *Lord of the Flies*

I don't understand why they call me Piggy. I'm not that fat am I? I miss my mom and dad. What are we supposed to do until we get saved? I'm cold and hungry, when are we going to eat? I hope no one expects me to find food, there's no way that I'm going into that jungle, I'm going to stay right here near the beach away from all the wild animals. I wonder why everyone is so mean to me? Maybe they have a problem. Yeah, what's their problem anyway?

Book used: Golding, W. (1959). *Lord of the flies.* Berkeley, CA: Berkley Publishing Group.

Contributed by Brooke Sibley, San Francisco, CA, Fall 2003.

How Else Can We Use This Strategy?

Sharing: The teacher may provide time for students to share with others what they have written.

Where Can We Learn More?

Clyde, J. A. (2003). Stepping inside the story world. *The Reading Teacher, 57,* 2–150.

Mantione, R. D., & Sabine, S. (2003). *Weaving through words: Using the arts to teach reading comprehension strategies.* Newark, DE: International Reading Association.

Mepham, J. *Interior monologue.* Retrieved March 3, 2005, from The Literacy Encyclopedia, http://www.litencyc.com/php/stopics

24

Jigsaw

Suggested Grade Levels: 3 to 8

Elements Addressed: Plot/theme, expository text

Meta-Strategies Incorporated: Determining important information, asking questions, summarizing and synthesizing

Supplies: A large or difficult text divided into approximately equal sections with one section for each group of students

WHAT IS JIGSAW? ●

Jigsaw is a cooperative strategy in which each student or group of students develops expertise about one section of a text and shares that expertise with others. Each student or student group provides one piece to the puzzle, or the complete literary work.

When Do We Use It?

This strategy works well for a large or difficult piece of text when time for working with it is limited. Students work on it as they read and complete the strategy after reading.

Why Do We Use It?

The jigsaw strategy requires students to master a section of text and to teach what they have learned to others. Students are often motivated to learn when they know that others depend on their expertise. Jigsaw is also a good strategy for exposing students to a large amount of material in a short time.

How Do We Use the Jigsaw Strategy?

Before introducing the unit to the class, the teacher divides the book into roughly equal sections. One "expert group" is then assigned to each section. After students have read their section, they discuss with other experts in their group, asking questions of each other and clarifying. Experts decide within their groups what information is important to share with others and how it should be presented. They make notes about their section, mark passages, and create sketches to share.

After students have read and mastered their sections, the class is reorganized into "home groups." Each home group has one expert on each section to be discussed. Students in the same home group sit around a table or in a circle facing each other. Students discuss the entire text, with each expert sharing the section studied in expert groups.

How Else Can We Use This Strategy?

Subject Matter Study: This strategy can be used to help students learn material for subjects such as science (e.g., the different types of rock) or social studies (e.g., the different continents or different wars).

Where Can We Learn More?

Aronson, E. (2000). *Social psychology network.* Retrieved from http://www.jig saw.org.

Aronson, E., & Patnoe, S. (1997). *The jigsaw classroom: Building cooperation in the classroom* (2nd ed.). New York: Addison Wesley Longman.

Aronson, E., & Yates, S. (1983). Cooperation in the classroom: The impact of the jigsaw method on inter-ethnic relations, classroom performance and self-esteem. In H. Blumberg & P. Hare (Eds.), *Small groups.* London: Wiley.

Clarke, J. (1994). Pieces of the puzzle: The jigsaw method. In S. Sharan (Ed.), *Handbook of cooperative learning methods.* Westport CT: Greenwood Press.

Hertz-Lazarowitz, R., Kagan, S., Sharan, S., Slavin, R., & Webb, C. (Eds.). (1985). *Learning to cooperate: Cooperating to learn.* New York: Plenum.

Kagan, S. (1992). *Cooperative learning.* San Juan Capistrano, CA: Kagan Cooperative Learning.

Figure 24.1 Jigsaw

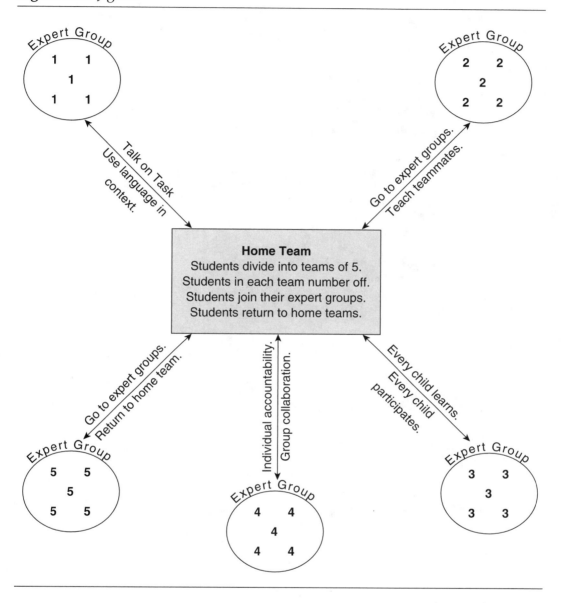

Figure 24.2

Jigsaw Discussion Sheet

Name: _____

Expert Group #: _____

Book: _____

Reading Assignment: page _____ to page _____

Everyone in your Expert Group is reading the same section of the book. To prepare for a good discussion, plan to share what you have learned and connect it with what others bring to the discussion. Make notes about and prepare for the following, either while you read or after you have finished reading.

Summary and Reactions

Main Idea:

_____

_____

One Interesting Idea:

_____

_____

Personal Reaction:

_____

_____

Mark some passages that you could read aloud to help other group members understand your section of the book.

Sketch a picture related to your reading. Draw something specifically from the text or something related to the text from own experience. Be prepared to show your picture and discuss it with your group.

Share your work and ideas with your Expert Group, and then in your Home Group.

Copyright © 2006 by Corwin Press. All rights reserved. Reprinted from *60 Strategies for Improving Reading Comprehension in Grades K – 8*, by Kathleen Feeney Jonson. Thousand Oaks, CA: Corwin Press, www.corwinpress.com. Reproduction authorized only for the local school site that has purchased this book.

25

K-W-L Chart

> Suggested Grade Levels: K to 8
>
> Elements Addressed: Character, expository text
>
> Meta-Strategies Incorporated: Asking questions, summarizing and synthesizing
>
> Supplies: Any expository text or fiction containing many facts, whiteboard or flipchart and dark-colored markers, lined paper; pencils

WHAT IS A K-W-L CHART?

K-W-L is an acronym for *know, want to know,* and *learned.* Students use a chart to record their ideas and questions before reading a selection and then to record what they have learned after reading.

Donna Ogle (1986), who first developed the K-W-L strategy, suggests that it is best suited for text containing factual information. It can also be used with fiction—but selectively. It would probably not be appropriate, for example, with a fantasy story in which animals talk.

When Do We Use It?

The K-W-L strategy is used before and after the reading process. Students fill out the first two columns of the chart ("know" and "want to know") before they begin reading literature containing factual information. They complete the third column ("learned") after they have read.

Why Do We Use It?

Using this strategy, students activate their current knowledge before reading. Next, they determine what they would like to learn, thereby establishing a purpose for reading. Finally, they reflect on what they have learned and summarize their understanding. This process helps them to become more actively engaged in their reading, organize their thoughts, put their knowledge in perspective, and integrate their new knowledge with prior knowledge. Students can later look back at these charts to review what they have learned.

How Do We Use K-W-L Charts?

Before reading, students create a chart with three columns, labeled (1) "What I Know," (2) "What I Want to Know," and (3) "What I Have Learned." Still before reading, they brainstorm what they know about the subject matter and write the information in the first column of the chart. In the second column, they write down what they would like to learn and expect to learn through their reading. The teacher may model this process on a whiteboard or flipchart before students begin their own charts.

As they read the book or section of the book—or just after they finish reading—students write in the third column what they have learned. Also, after they finish reading, they cross out or write notes next to any information in the first column that was incorrect. By organizing their thoughts in this way, students document their growing understanding of a topic.

How Else Can We Use This Strategy?

K-W-L-S: Students use a fourth column, labeled "Still Want to Know," to list unanswered questions that they would like to research further.

K-W-H-L: Students use a four-column chart to help access prior information. The K-W-L are the same as for the K-W-L chart. The H column is for students to note *how* they can find out what they want to learn.

K-T-W-L: Students use this organizer to help predict and connect prior knowledge. K-T-W-L stands for *what I Know, what I Think I know, what I Want to know,* and *what I Learned.*

KWL Flipchart: Using the format of the K-W-L chart, students make individual flipcharts. They fold paper in half, top to bottom, and then cut the top section into three flaps and label the outsides of the flaps "K," "W," and "L." Next, they lift the flaps and write their ideas on the paper beneath. By raising the flaps, they can look at the columns one at a time.

Alternative Wording: Instead of the previously discussed headings, columns are titled "I Understand," "I Don't Understand," and "I Wonder."

Group Chart: A whole class or a small group of students work together on this activity, displaying their ideas on a board or chart paper. This works well for younger children.

Affect: A fourth column is added to the chart for students to record how the information affects them. In this column, students record their personal responses to the information they have learned.

Small-Group Study: Groups of students focus on different aspects of the book. Each group completes a chart specific to its subject area.

K-W-L Plus: After creating the K-W-L chart, students map what they have listed in their "L" column, with the main topic in the middle and with major concepts and important details stemming from the topic. Then they write a summary of what they have learned. This incorporates tools of restructuring text and rewriting information to help students process it.

Where Can We Learn More?

Bryan, J. (1998). K-W-W-L: Questioning the known. *The Reading Teacher, 51*(7).

Mandeville, T. F. (1994). KWLA: Linking the affective and cognitive domains. *The Reading Teacher, 47,* 679–680.

McLaughlin, M., & Allen, B. A. (2002). *Guided comprehension: A teaching model for grades 3–8.* Newark, DE: International Reading Association.

Ogle, D. M. (1986). K.-W.-L.: A teaching model that develops active reading of expository text. *The Reading Teacher, 39,* 564–570.

Ogle, D. M. (1989). *The know, want to know, learn strategy.* In K. D. Muth (Ed.), *Children's comprehension of text: Research into practice* (pp. 205–223). Newark, DE: International Reading Association.

Schmidt, P. R. (1999). KWLQ: Inquiry and literacy learning in science. *The Reading Teacher, 52*(7).

Sippola, A. E. (1995). K-W-L-S. *The Reading Teacher, 48*(6).

Tarquin, P., & Walker, S. (1997). *Creating success in the classroom! Visual organizers and how to use them.* Portsmouth, NH: Teacher Ideas Press/Libraries Unlimited.

Tompkins, G. E. (2004). *Fifty literacy strategies: Step by step. (2nd ed.)* Upper Saddle River, NJ: Prentice Hall.

Weissman, K. E. (1996). Using paragraph frames to complete a KWL. *The Reading Teacher, 50*(3).

Yopp, R. H., & Yopp, H. K. (2001). *Literature-based reading activities* (3rd ed.). Boston: Allyn & Bacon.

Figure 25.1

K-W-L Chart

Based on *Amazing Grace*

What We (I) Know	What We (I) Want To Know	What We (I) Learned
Amazing Grace is a song Amazing means something extra special or extraordinary Grace can be someone's name The girl on the cover of the book is African American	If the book is about the girl on the cover, why is she amazing? Is her name Grace? Does she have brothers or sisters?	Grace was the main character in the book. She was amazing because she did what she believed in, no matter what anyone said. She lived with her mother and grandmother. She did not have any brothers or sisters.

Book used: Hoffman, M. (1991). *Amazing Grace.* New York: Dial Books for Younger Readers, Penguin.

Contributed by Kate Working, San Francisco, CA, Fall 2003.

Figure 25.2

K-W-L Chart

Based on a Nonfiction Book about Whales

What I Already Know	What I Want To Know	What I Have Learned
Whales are very big. Their blubber keeps them warm in the ocean.	1. How much do they weigh? 2. How do whales breathe? 3. How many babies at one time can they have?	1. They can weigh up to 180 tons. 2. Whales have lungs and must come to the surface to breathe. 3. They can have one baby at one time.

Contributed by Julie Walton, San Francisco, CA, Fall 2003.

Figure 25.3

KWHL Chart

Moscow, Russia

K What we already know:	W What we want to find out:	H How we will find out:	L What we learned:
Moscow is the capital of Russia.	How people make a living in Moscow.	Read books about Moscow and Russia.	Moscow was founded in A.D.1147.
It used to be the capital of the Soviet Union.	Why churches in Moscow have onion-shaped domes.	Look in an encyclopedia.	The city has burned down and been rebuilt many times.
It is very cold in Moscow for a lot of the year.	Why people in Moscow have to stand in line so much.	Watch a video about Moscow.	Many people work for the government.
Moscow is very large.	Where people live.	Talk to people who have visited Moscow.	Most families live crowded together in small apartments.
	What people do for fun.		People enjoy Moscow's parks, circuses, chess, & ballets.
	How old Moscow is.		

26

Learning Logs

Suggested Grade Levels: K to 8

Elements Addressed: Plot/theme, character, expository text

Meta-Strategies Incorporated: Monitoring reading for meaning (clarifying), determining important information, summarizing and synthesizing

Supplies: Narrative or expository text or a series of texts, a notebook for each student, pens or pencils

WHAT IS A LEARNING LOG? ●

A learning log is a journal in which students make notes, record observations, and reflect on their reading. It may include illustrations.

When Do We Use It?

Students may write in their learning log every day, several times per week, or weekly.

Why Do We Use It?

Learning logs offer students the opportunity to clarify their thinking, make connections, and reflect on their reading. Using their logs, students may also initiate ideas for larger writing projects.

How Do We Use Learning Logs?

On a regular basis—daily or weekly, for example—students write in their learning logs. They may be instructed to write about a certain topic or a piece of literature read that day, or they may have the opportunity to write whatever they like. They write freely, without polishing their prose. Charts, drawings, and freewriting are all acceptable.

Teachers review the logs periodically and learn from them how well students understand their reading. Learning logs are generally marked on a credit/no credit basis. The teacher writes comments in the log but does not grade it.

How Else Can We Use This Strategy?

Creative Logs: At the beginning of a unit, students create their own learning logs from lined paper, with construction paper covers. Students may be creative in designing their cover.

Where Can We Learn More?

Bromley, K. (1993). Journaling: Engagements in reading, writing, and thinking. In *Teaching Strategies.* New York: Scholastic.

Cooper, J. D. (2006). *Literacy: Helping children construct meaning.* Boston: Houghton Mifflin.

Thompson, A. (1990). Thinking and writing with learning logs. In N. Atwell (Ed.), *Coming to know: Writing to learn in the intermediate grades* (pp. 35–51). Portsmouth, NH: Heinemann.

Tompkins, G. E. (1994). *Teaching writing: Balancing process and product* (2nd ed.). Upper Saddle River, NJ: Merrill/Prentice Hall.

Tompkins, G. E. (2004). *Fifty literacy strategies: Step by step* (2nd ed.). Upper Saddle River, NJ: Pearson-Prentice Hall.

Figure 26.1

www.coachart.org

Journal Entry
Friday, December 5, 2003

Topic: Describe something you feel
passionate about and why.

I am passionate about CoachArt, the
nonprofit organization that my oldest
brother founded in honor of our father
who passed away in December of 1996.
CoachArt provides life-enhancing extra-
curricular activities to children and
teenagers who have been afflicted with
life-threatening illness. CoachArt matches
CoachArt kids with coaches, tutors and
mentors in their area who possess the
expertise in the activity of their choice.
Those activities include music, drama, art,
sports, dance, yoga, photography, creative writing
and more. These lessons are free to the kids
and help bring normalcy and happiness to their
lives. I am proud of CoachArt's mission, to be
the sister of the founder, and the daughter
of the person whom the organization is founded
in honor of. It feels right to participate in a
cause that does so much good for those who
need help most.

Music
lessons!
-guitar
-piano
-violin
-flute
-saxaphone

painting!

creative
writing!

SPORTS!

Contributed by Eliza Lurie, San Francisco, CA, Fall 2003.

27

Life Experience

> Also Called: Making a Personal Connection
>
> Suggested Grade Levels: K to 8
>
> Elements Addressed: Plot/theme, character, expository text
>
> Meta-Strategies Incorporated: Making connections, visualizing
>
> Supplies: Narrative or expository text, lined paper, pens or pencils

● WHAT IS LIFE EXPERIENCE?

For the life experience strategy, students use quickwriting to relate a book or story to personal experience.

When Do We Use It?

This strategy works well before students begin or after they have finished reading.

Why Do We Use It?

Life experience encourages students to make personal connections between their lives and the lives of characters they are reading about. It helps students understand that literature explores universal truths.

How Do We Use the Life Experience Strategy?

The teacher identifies a theme in the literature and asks students to quickwrite about a personal experience related to the selected theme. Possible themes include the first day of school, prejudice, friendship, or a holiday experience. After quickwriting, students discuss their experiences and the connection to the literature.

Figure 27.1   Personal Connection (Life Experience) Worksheet

Personal Connections

Title of Book: _____ Your Name _____ Date _____

While reading, put a sticky note at a place where you connect your own life to the text. Think about your past experiences and prior knowledge. In the space below, copy the words or explain or draw the picture, and write down your connection.

Quote or Picture from Text

This reminds me of . . .

Quote or Picture from Text

This reminds me of . . .

Copyright © 2006 by Corwin Press. All rights reserved. Reprinted from *60 Strategies for Improving Reading Comprehension in Grades K – 8*, by Kathleen Feeney Jonson. Thousand Oaks, CA: Corwin Press, www.corwinpress.com. Reproduction authorized only for the local school site that has purchased this book.

How Else Can We Use This Strategy?

Beginning Readers: Children in the earlier grades may discuss their experiences rather than writing about them.

Where Can We Learn More?

Christen, W. L., & Murphy, T. J. (1991). Increasing comprehension by activating prior knowledge. *ERIC Digest on Reading, English, and Communication.* East Lansing, MI: National Center for Research on Teacher Learning. (ERIC Document Reproduction Service No. ED. 328885).

Harvey, S., & Goudvis, A. (2000). Making connections: A bridge from the new to the known. In S. Harvey, A. Goudvis, & P. Stratton (Eds.), *Strategies that work: Teaching comprehension to enhance understanding* (pp. 67–75, 266–269). Portland, ME: Stenhouse.

Keene, E. O., & Zimmerman, S. (1997). Homes in the mind: Connecting the known to the new. In E. O. Keene (Ed.), *Mosaic of thought: Teaching comprehension in a reader's workshop* (pp. 45–71). Portsmouth, NH: Heinemann.

28

Literacy Quilt

Suggested Grade Levels: K to 8

Elements Addressed: Plot/theme, character

Meta-Strategies Incorporated: Determining important information, summarizing and synthesizing

Supplies: Narrative text, 5-inch-by-5-inch squares of colored construction paper, construction paper scraps, glue stick, scissors, pencils, markers, butcher paper, and masking tape or stapler and staples

WHAT IS A LITERACY QUILT?

A literacy quilt is a collection of paper squares created by students who have read the same piece of literature. Each square illustrates some theme or favorite part of a text. The taped-together squares make up a "quilt" that reveals the class depiction of the text.

When Do We Use It?

This strategy works best after students have completed their reading.

Why Do We Use It?

Quilt squares highlight the most important events and characters in a story and creatively summarize the text. They can be used to highlight themes as well. Quilts provide a fun way for kids to use artwork in their literature study. They can also be used to celebrate a recently completed book.

How Do We Use Literacy Quilts?

The teacher gives each student one 5-inch-by-5-inch construction paper square. Students also receive an assortment of paper scraps, which they tear or cut into pieces and glue to their square to create an image that they feel is important to the story. The image may represent a theme, a character, or the setting. On the bottom of the square, students write a name, word, or sentence to label their image.

After all squares are completed, the teacher or a group of students tapes the backs of the squares together and attaches the squares to butcher paper backing. Alternatively, the teacher may staple the squares next to each other on a bulletin board. The entire quilt is displayed in the classroom.

How Else Can We Use This Strategy?

Text Quotations: Instead of labeling squares, students add a quotation from the text.

Creative Quilts: A more elaborate design than simple squares is used to create the quilt.

Where Can We Learn More?

Buchberg, W. (1999). *Quilting across the curriculum (grades 1–3).* New York: Scholastic.

Cobb, M. (1995). *The quilt-block history of pioneer days with projects kids can make.* Brookfield, CT: Millbrook.

Tompkins, G. E. (1998). *Language arts: Content and teaching strategies* (4th ed.). Upper Saddle River, NJ: Prentice Hall.

Tompkins, G. E. (2004). *Fifty literacy strategies: Step by step* (2nd ed.). Upper Saddle River, NJ: Pearson-Prentice Hall.

Whitford, P. A. (1996). *Eight hands round: A patchwork alphabet.* New York: Harper Trophy.

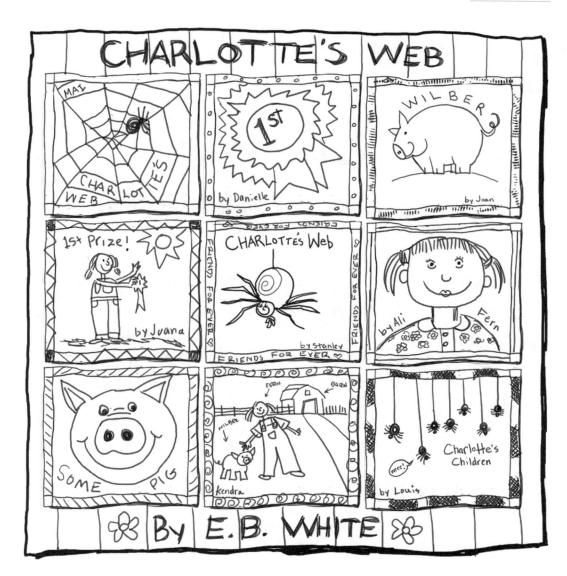

29

Literary Sociogram

Suggested Grade Levels: 6 to 8

Elements Addressed: Character

Meta-Strategies Incorporated: Monitoring reading for meaning (clarifying)

Supplies: Any text with several characters, large sheets of drawing paper, pencils with erasers

● WHAT IS A LITERARY SOCIOGRAM?

A literary sociogram is a graphic representation of relationships and feelings among characters in a story.

When Do We Use It?

The sociogram is particularly useful if students work on it at various times as they read a piece of literature.

Why Do We Use It?

The sociogram forces students to think about relationships among characters and helps readers to understand those relationships. This strategy draws on literal, inferential, and evaluative thinking. The thinking process required for this strategy is most important; the end product is secondary.

How Do We Use Literary Sociograms?

Because this is a difficult but valuable strategy, the teacher first leads the class as a group in developing sociograms based on several different pieces of literature. Only after completing several group samples are students asked to create their own sociograms.

Students may want to work in pairs on this project. When they work together, they must discuss their ideas. They should come up with creative, original ways to show relationships among characters.

In *Literacy Through Literature,* Terry Johnson and Daphne Louis (1988) give the following tips for making a sociogram:

1. Begin by placing the central character or characters in the center of a piece of paper. Draw a line to divide the paper in half, with the line passing through the central character.

2. Add other characters around the central characters. Put characters supporting the main character on one side of a dividing line and those against the main character on the other side. This divides the characters into "good guys" and "bad guys."

3. Place characters who are closer psychologically to the main character closer to the character on the paper.

4. Make the most important, most powerful characters larger than less important, less powerful characters.

5. Draw arrows between the characters. Use solid lines to represent substantiated relationships and broken lines to represent inferred relationships. Point the arrow in the direction of the relationship.

6. Add words to label relationships.

7. Circle active characters with a solid line. Circle characters who are significantly absent (such as dead characters) with a broken line.

For this strategy to be effective, students must have the opportunity to revise their work as they read through the literature and learn more about the characters.

How Else Can We Use This Strategy?

Points in Time: Students make different sociograms to reflect character relationships at different points in the story.

Where Can We Learn More?

Johnson, T. D., & Louis, D. R. (1988). *Literacy through literature.* Portsmouth, NH: Heinemann.

Johnson, T. D., & Louis, D. R. (1989). *Bringing it all together: A program for literacy.* Portsmouth, NH: Heinemann.

Pappas, C. C., Kiefer, B. Z., & Levstik, L. S. (1999). *An integrated language perspective in the elementary school: An action approach* (3rd ed.). New York: Addison Wesley Longman.

Figure 29.1 Sample Sociogram based on *Alexander and the Terrible, Horrible, No Good, Very Bad Day*

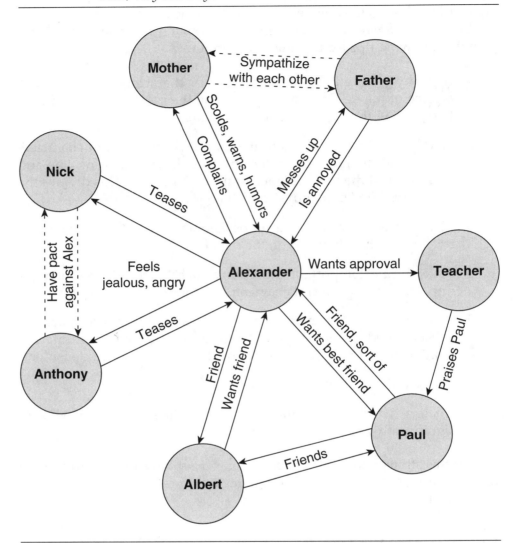

Book Used: Viorst, J. (1972). *Alexander and the Terrible, Horrible, No Good, Very Bad Day*. Authenem.

30

Literature Circles

> Suggested Grade Levels: 3 to 8
>
> Elements Addressed: Plot/theme, character
>
> Meta-Strategies Incorporated: Making connections, monitoring reading for meaning (clarifying), determining important information, visualizing, asking questions, making inferences, summarizing and synthesizing
>
> Supplies: Assorted books, lined paper or a notebook for each student, pens or pencils

WHAT IS A LITERATURE CIRCLE? ●

A literature circle is a small group of students who all read the same text and then meet to discuss and respond to it. Harvey Daniels (1994) has been credited with developing the major reference for the strategy in his book, *Literature Circles: Voice and Choice in the Student-Centered Classroom.*

When Do We Use It?

Literature circles can be used before reading begins to get students excited about a book. They can also be used throughout the reading process and after students have finished the book.

Why Do We Use It?

Literature circles allow students to work together with other students. Students lead the process, taking ownership of their discussion.

How Do We Use Literature Circles?

The teacher introduces five or six books of various lengths and reading levels. A sign-up sheet is made available with a limited number of spaces for each book—perhaps up to five or six students per book. Students should be warned that they may not get to read their first-choice book.

After students have selected a book, all of those who have chosen the same book are assigned to the same group. Some adjustments may be necessary to create groups of similar sizes. Students then have time to read in class or take the book home to read. As they read, they take notes, recording their observations, thoughts, and questions.

After each section of reading, students meet in their groups to discuss their notes and observations. They ask questions of each other and make predictions about later parts of the book. They then repeat the process, reading more and then discussing more. After groups have completely finished their books, they may present what they have read to the class.

How Else Can We Use This Strategy?

Question Sheets: Students complete in-depth question sheets as they read. They then use these sheets to spark discussion in their groups.

Student Roles: Each student is assigned a role for each group meeting. For example,

- One student, the discussion director, comes up with questions to get the group talking.
- One student, the word wizard, chooses vocabulary words to share and discuss.
- One student, the passage master, selects three or four short passages and reads them aloud.
- One student, the connector, makes connections to his or her personal life.
- One student, the illustrator, draws a picture or diagram related to the reading.

Each time the group meets, students take different roles.

Reading Levels: Instead of choosing books, students are assigned to books based on reading level. This enables students to work with other students of relatively equal ability.

Where Can We Learn More?

Cornett, C. E. (1997). Beyond retelling the plot: Student-led discussions. *Teaching Reading, 6,* 527–528.

Daniels, H. (1994). *Literature circles: Voice and choice in the student-centered classroom.* York, ME: Stenhouse.

Daniels, H. (2003). The literature circle: Reading like a writer. *Voices from the Middle, 11*(2) (December), 58–59.

Peterson, R., & Eeds, M. (1990). *Grand conversations: Literature groups in action.* New York: Scholastic.

Yopp, R. H., & Yopp, H. K. (2001). *Literature-based reading activities* (3rd ed.). Boston: Allyn & Bacon.

Figure 30.1

Literature Circles

Possible Roles for Participants

Each student in each group is assigned one role for literature circles. Possible roles are

- **Discussion director**

- **Word wizard**

- **Passage master**

- **Connector**

- **Illustrator**

Following are sample worksheets for each of these roles, with explanations of the participant's responsibilities and with guidelines for preparation.

(Continued)

TOURO COLLEGE LIBRARY

Figure 30.1 (Continued)

Student Role for Literature Circles

Discussion Director

Name: _____

Book: _____

Pages: _____

Job: Write a list of questions that your group might want to talk about (discuss). Try to make your questions FAT questions—not about small details. Some of the best questions have to do with your thoughts and feelings as you read the story. List your questions here:

1. _____

   _____

2. _____

   _____

3. _____

   _____

(See next page for suggested questions.)

Sample questions for Discussion Director:

<u>To focus on **theme:**</u> What lesson does the story teach? What's the story about? Does it remind you of another story?

<u>To focus on **author:**</u> What do you think the author is saying? Why did the author write this book? What did the author need to know? What's special about the author's writing?

<u>To focus on **plot:**</u> What problems do the characters face? How are they solved? How would you solve these problems?

<u>To focus on **language:**</u> Does the author do a good job painting pictures in your head with words? Find two interesting sentences or phrases to share, and mark them with sticky notes.

<u>To focus on **mood:**</u> Choose a scene that made you happy or sad. Does it remind you of something that happened to you? What was the most exciting part?

<u>To focus on **illustrations:**</u> Choose one or two pictures to share. Tell why you chose them. How might you change them and why?

<u>To focus on **place:**</u> Where does the story take place? What words does the author use to describe the place? How do the pictures tell about the place?

<u>To focus on **characters:**</u> Choose one character and mark with sticky notes how he or she looks, talks, and behaves. Does the character remind you of someone you know? Would you like to be that character?

(Continued)

Figure 30.1 (Continued)

Student Role for Literature Circles

Word Wizard

Name: _____

Book: _____

Pages: _____

Job: Look out for interesting words in the reading. If you find words that you don't know, mark them and their page number and then later look up their definitions. You might also find words that you know but that are used in strange ways. Write them down, too, with their page numbers.

Page # and Paragraph	Word	Definition
_____	_____	_____
		_____
		_____
_____	_____	_____
		_____
_____	_____	_____
		_____
		_____
_____	_____	_____
		_____

Student Role for Literature Circles

Passage Master

Name: _____

Book: _____

Pages: _____

Job: Find a few special sections in the book that you like and that you think the group should take a look at. Possible reasons for choosing a passage are here:

Important	**Surprising**
Very Descriptive	**Confusing**
Funny	**Scary**

Location: Reason for Picking:

page _____, paragraph _____   _____

_____

page _____, paragraph _____   _____

_____

page _____, paragraph _____   _____

_____

(Continued)

Figure 30.1 (Continued)

Student Role for Literature Circles

Connector

Name: _____

Book: _____

Pages: _____

Job: Find things in the reading that remind you of your life or of the way the world is. Find *people* who are like people you know or have heard about. Find *places* that are like a place you know or have heard about. Find *problems* that remind you of a real-life problem you've had or heard about. Tell how the book reminded you of that person, place, or problem.

1. _____

   _____

2. _____

   _____

3. _____

   _____

4. _____

   _____

Student Role for Literature Circles

Illustrator

Name: _____

Book: _____

Pages: _____

Job: Draw a picture that has to do with the reading. You can draw something that happened in the story, something the story reminds you of, or something that shows the feelings you had reading the book. You can label your drawing with words if that helps. You may use the back of this paper.

Presenting Your Picture: First show your picture to everyone in the group, asking each group member to tell you what he or she thinks the picture means. At the end, tell what your picture is about.

Daniels, H. (1994). *Literature circles: Voice and choice in the student-centered classroom.* York, ME: Stenhouse.

31

Mind Mapping

Also Called: Clustering, Idea Mapping

Suggested Grade Levels: K to 8

Elements Addressed: Plot/theme, character, expository text

Meta-Strategies Incorporated: Monitoring reading for meaning (clarifying), determining important information

Supplies: Narrative or expository text, drawing paper, colored pencils or markers

WHAT IS MIND MAPPING? ●

Mind mapping is a graphic depiction of relationships among aspects of a text. Students use symbols and words to draw relationships and determine how minor incidents relate to major themes.

When Do We Use It?

Mind mapping is a good brainstorming strategy and a technique for organizing information after students have completed reading but before they begin to write. Students may also use mind mapping while reading a piece of literature to help them organize their ideas.

Why Do We Use It?

Mind mapping helps students to structure their ideas. Using this technique, they make connections, realize relationships, look further into things, and analyze what they are reading.

How Do We Use Mind Mapping?

This strategy works best if the teacher first models it, leading the class in creating a map as a group. After students have worked through the process one or more times, they create individual maps.

To begin, students draw a geometric shape—a square, circle, or rectangle—and write a main idea or thesis within the shape. Next they draw lines extending from the center shape and write supporting ideas on those lines. Students cluster ideas around the main point based on relationships they determine. They use colored pencils or markers to categorize related ideas.

How Else Can We Use This Strategy?

Character Map: Students analyze characters within a piece of literature.

Narrative Summary: Students begin with the main event from a piece of literature as the center of the map. On the lines, they write incidents that relate to the main event.

Where Can We Learn More?

Ekhaml, L. (1998). Graphic organizers: Outlets for your thoughts. *School Library Media Activities Monthly, 14*, 29–33.

Goodnough, K., & Long, R. (2002). Mind mapping: A graphic organizer for the pedagogical toolbox. *Science Scope, 25*, 8–20.

Hyerle, D. (1996). *Visual tools for constructing knowledge.* Alexandria, VA: Association for Supervision and Curriculum Development.

Lazear, D. (1991). *Seven ways of teaching: The artistry of teaching with multiple intelligences.* Palatine, IL: Skylight.

Margulies, N. (1991). *Mapping inner space: Learning and teaching mind mapping.* Tucson, AZ: Zephyr Press.

Figure 31.1   3rd Grade Students' Map Based on Story Read Aloud in Class

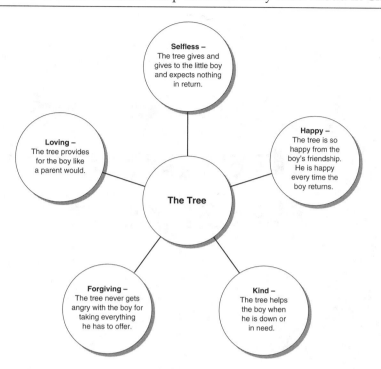

Book used: Silverstein, S. (1964). *The giving tree.* New York: HarperCollins.

Contributed by Stephanie Abramowitz, San Francisco, CA, Fall 2003.

Figure 31.2   High School Students' Map Based on History Textbook

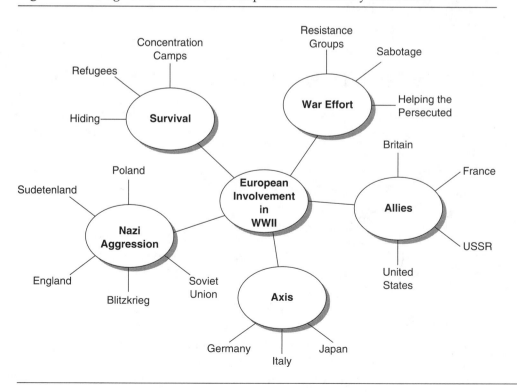

32

Open Mind Character Analysis

Also Called: Mindscape

Suggested Grade Levels: 3 to 8

Elements Addressed: Character

Meta-Strategies Incorporated: Monitoring reading for meaning, determining important information

Supplies: Narrative or expository text (especially good with fiction and biography); open mind template or sample and blank drawing paper; pencils, colored pencils, or markers

● WHAT IS OPEN MIND CHARACTER ANALYSIS?

The open mind is a diagram used as a brainstorming tool for students to analyze a character visually. Students write words and/or draw pictures to represent the character's thoughts and feelings within an outline of a person's mind.

When Do We Use It?

Open mind character analysis can be used effectively during or immediately after reading a piece of literature. It works particularly well as a prewriting or prediscussion strategy to get students to think about characters.

Why Do We Use It?

This exercise helps students to focus their understanding of a specific character and to see things from that character's point of view. When they draw symbols associated with the character, students improve their visual understanding. When they verbalize thoughts, they focus their ideas and make interpretive connections.

The open mind strategy helps students to put themselves in the role of a character, develop perspective, think about a character's motivations and thoughts, and use writing and/or symbols to represent their thinking. It prepares students to talk or write about a character.

English language learners can use illustrations and symbols to build their thoughts even before they have developed adequate vocabulary.

How Do We Use Open Mind Character Analysis?

This strategy is best modeled before students create their own open mind graphic. A large outline of a head (representing an open mind) is displayed before the class. The students either are assigned or choose a character and are told to imagine that they are that character. The teacher may ask them to focus on a specific time or event in the book.

The teacher or a student recorder begins by writing the name of the character above the character's head. Students then suggest symbols, pictures, words, or phrases to go inside the head to illustrate the character's internal thoughts, emotions, and reactions: what that character is thinking about; what the character's priorities are; and the character's self-perceptions, thoughts, fears, and hopes. Phrases may be quoted from the text or may be in the student's own words. Older students use complete sentences outside of the diagram to explain the rationale behind the symbols and phrases.

After this sample group effort, the teacher passes out copies of a paper with an outline of a head drawn on it or tells students to draw their own outline on a blank sheet of paper. Then students are instructed to choose their own character and create an open mind character analysis of that character.

How Else Can We Use This Strategy?

Two Heads: Students create two open minds to show the differences between characters.

Point in Time: Students create open mind portraits for the same character at different times in the book and then compare and contrast the different analyses of the same character.

Partner Sharing: Students share their open mind drawings with a partner.

Where Can We Learn More?

Clyde, J. A. (2003). Stepping inside the story world. *The Reading Teacher, 57,* 2–150.

Curran, C. E. (1997). Analyzing story characters: Facilitating higher level comprehension skills in students with learning disabilities. *Intervention in School and Clinic, 32*(5), 312–315.

Geli, J. A. (1998). Actor's studio comes to the classroom: Character analysis in literature. *Exercise Exchange, 43*(2), 8–9.

Johannessen, L. R. (2001). Enhancing response to literature through character analysis. *Clearing House, 74*(3), 145–150.

Tompkins, G. E. (2003). *Literacy for the twenty-first century: A balanced approach* (3rd ed.). Upper Saddle River, NJ: Merrill/Prentice Hall.

Tompkins, G. E. (2004). *Fifty literacy strategies: Step by step* (2nd ed.). Upper Saddle River, NJ: Pearson-Prentice Hall.

Figure 32.1

Book used: Park, B. (2001). *Junie B. First Grader (at Last!).* New York: Random House. Contributed by Stephanie Abramowitz, San Francisco, CA, Fall 2003.

Figure 32.2

Copyright © 2006 by Corwin Press. All rights reserved. Reprinted from *60 Strategies for Improving Reading Comprehension in Grades K – 8*, by Kathleen Feeney Jonson. Thousand Oaks, CA: Corwin Press, www.corwinpress. com. Reproduction authorized only for the local school site that has purchased this book.

33

Paired Retellings

Suggested Grade Levels: K to 8

Elements Addressed: Plot/theme, character, expository text

Meta-Strategies Incorporated: Determining important information, summarizing and synthesizing

Supplies: Narrative or expository text, retelling worksheets (one for each student), pens or pencils

● WHAT IS PAIRED RETELLING?

Paired retelling is a strategy used by students working in dyads. Students retell, in their own words, a selection of text to their partner. During some paired retellings, the teacher provides a *retelling guide* specific to the story or text selection.

When Do We Use It?

This strategy is used after students have read a selection of text or a complete story.

Why Do We Use It?

Before they can retell something in their own words, students must evaluate the original text and understand it. The process of retelling in turn reinforces student understanding and enhances student comprehension and recall.

How Do We Use Paired Retellings?

To model this strategy, the teacher selects a piece of text that the students have read or (for younger students) heard. The text may be either narrative or expository. Often the teacher practices retelling the material before presenting it to the class. Then the teacher *retells* the events in the text, while students make notes on the record form. The teacher could leave out important information as he or she retells the text so that students realize that their partners may miss significant details as they retell what they have read.

The teacher then explains to students that reciting content, using their own words as much as possible, is a good way for them to make sure they understand and can remember what they have read. Retellings may focus on characters, setting and events of a narrative, or important details of expository writing.

To begin the activity, students pair up in teams of retellers and listeners. In their pairs, students read silently. When both have finished reading, one partner retells the passage in his or her own words. The listener marks with checks on the form the details the partner retells from the text. The listener uses the retelling guide provided by the teacher (either narrative or informational, as appropriate). These guides can be specific to a particular story or text, or generic in nature to fit any story. If the reteller has trouble remembering the story, the listener may ask questions to prompt a specific reply, for instance, "Do you remember the part where . . . ?" Retellers and listeners can switch roles so each has an opportunity to orally review the reading assignment.

When all students have completed their retellings and forms, the class has a group discussion about the content of the reading (major points) as well as the retelling process (e.g., what did they do if their partner jumped around in his or her retelling? what did they do if their partner became stuck? what follow-up questions did they discuss?). The teacher explains that retelling is a good strategy for students to use with *all* reading. They may retell what they have read to a partner, recite it for themselves, or even rewrite in their own words.

Figure 33.1

Paired Retelling

My Name: _____ Date: _____

I listened to: _____

Circle whether the book was fiction or nonfiction. Then put a mark by one or more things your partner did well:

Fiction   **Nonfiction**

My partner told me about   My partner told me about

_____ The characters.   _____ The main ideas.

_____ The setting.   _____ The details.

_____ The events in the story.

_____ The beginning.

_____ The ending.

Now retell the selection in your own words in the space here:

Copyright © 2006 by Corwin Press. All rights reserved. Reprinted from *60 Strategies for Improving Reading Comprehension in Grades K – 8*, by Kathleen Feeney Jonson. Thousand Oaks, CA: Corwin Press, www.corwinpress. com. Reproduction authorized only for the local school site that has purchased this book.

Figure 33.2

RETELLING GUIDE
for *Grandfather's Journey* by Allen Say

Directions: As your partner retells the story, put a check mark by the items remembered from the story. If he/she gets stuck, you may give one of the statements as a "prompt" or ask them a question related to the statement (i.e. "What do you remember about _____?") Put a "P" by any statements you provide for the reteller. The reteller does not have to tell the story in correct order. The reteller may jump around. If he or she gives you information not included with the statements below, put check marks at the end of the sentence where the information fits best. Specific supporting details are indented under a main idea.

_____ Grandfather left his home in Japan to see the world.

        _____ He went by boat

        _____ He didn't see land for three weeks.

_____ Grandfather explored the "New World" - North America.

        _____ traveled by train and river boat

        _____ saw many things
                _____ deserts and rocks
                _____ farmlands
                _____ huge cities
                _____ mountains and rivers

_____ He met many different kinds and colors of people.

_____ He liked California best of all the places he visited.

_____ He went back home to marry his childhood sweetheart.

_____ Grandfather and his bride came back to America.

        _____ They had a baby girl.

_____ Grandfather became homesick for Japan and wanted to return to his homeland.

_____ Grandfather returned to Japan, his first home, with his family.

        _____ moved to a big city

        _____ raised birds

        _____ a war came

        _____ his daughter married and had a son.

_____ Grandfather told his grandson many stories about California.

_____ Grandfather died before he could return to California.

_____ His grandson (the author) moved to California, but still misses Japan - just like his grandfather did.

From: Schulz, A. R. (1998). *Supporting intermediate and secondary readers: Selected interactive approaches*. Costa Mesa, CA: California Reading Association. Used with permission of California Reading Association.

How Else Can We Use This Strategy?

Written Retelling: Instead of reciting a passage for a partner, students close their books and rewrite the material from memory, in their own words.

Where Can We Learn More?

Koskinen, P. S., Gambrell, L. G., Kapinus, B., & Heathington, B. (1988). Retelling: A strategy for enhancing students' reading comprehension. *The Reading Teacher, 41*(9), 892–896.

Schulz, A. R. (1998). *Supporting intermediate and secondary readers: Selected interactive approaches.* Costa Mesa, CA: California Reading Association.

34

Pick-A-Pal

Suggested Grade Levels: K to 2

Elements Addressed: Character

Meta-Strategies Incorporated: Making connections, summarizing and synthesizing

Supplies: Narrative text, whiteboard or chart paper and dark-colored markers, drawing paper, colored pencils or markers, pens or pencils

---

WHAT IS PICK-A-PAL? ●

Pick-a-pal is a strategy in which younger students choose a character they would like as a best friend and explore qualities of that character.

When Do We Use It?

Students choose their pal after reading a selection or a complete text. They then complete the activity.

Why Do We Use It?

Pick-a-pal requires students to think carefully about the characters in their reading and to explore which characters they might like, what those characters look like, and how they might act.

How Do We Use the Pick-a-Pal Strategy?

The teacher introduces this strategy by having students brainstorm to come up with the names of several characters from stories read to and/or by the class recently. Through this brainstorming exercise, students review stories and characters from read-alouds, basal stories, and any other literature the class has experienced. The teacher lists the characters on a board or chart paper.

Next, students are asked to choose a character they would like to have as a best friend and are given time to draw a picture of that character. When they have finished, a volunteer holds up a picture of a "pal," and the class guesses which character is represented. After the class guesses, the student explains why that character would be a special pal. Other volunteers hold up their pictures and discuss their characters.

Each student then writes the name of the selected pal on the back of the picture and also writes a paragraph about what makes the character a good friend. Younger children or struggling readers may simply list adjectives or short phrases as explanations for liking the character. Pictures may be displayed on a class bulletin board.

How Else Can We Use This Strategy?

Follow-Up: Work created for pick-a-pal is saved in a portfolio. The strategy is used again late in the year and the student's growth noted in a comparison of two efforts.

Where Can We Learn More?

Curran, C. E. (1997). Analyzing story characters: Facilitating higher level comprehension skills in students with learning disabilities. *Intervention in School and Clinic, 32*(5), 312–315.

Johannessen, L. R. (2001). Enhancing response to literature through character analysis. *Clearing House, 74*(3), 145–150.

35

Plot Profile

Also Called: Time and Excitement Chart

Suggested Grade Levels: 3 to 8

Elements Addressed: Plot/theme

Meta-Strategies Incorporated: Determining important information, summarizing and synthesizing

Supplies: A chapter book with a strong plot, graph paper, pens or pencils

WHAT IS A PLOT PROFILE? ●

A plot profile is a graphic depiction of tension, or level of excitement, in each chapter of a story. Using the profile, students follow the sequence of events and tension from conflict.

When Do We Use It?

Students plot the tension in a book after each chapter. They analyze the profile after completing the book.

Why Do We Use It?

The plot profile enables readers to see the high and low tension of a book's plot. It helps students to see how the author develops structure, using conflict to build a plot.

How Do We Use Plot Profiles?

Before beginning this strategy, the teacher leads a discussion about plot and conflict and explains how tension keeps the reader interested. Terms such as *problem, conflict,* and *resolution* are discussed. Next, the class talks about different types of conflict and the excitement conflict brings to a story. Then, still before beginning a novel, each student receives a sheet of graph paper on which to plot the action. In the left margin, starting at the top, students write the following words to record tension level vertically: "Edge of your seat," "Can't put it down," "Moderate," "Calm," and "Dull." Horizontally, at the bottom, students designate one line for each chapter of the book.

Students begin reading. At the end of each chapter, they are asked to plot the tension at that point in the story. After they have finished reading the book, students explain their justification for determining levels of tension. They talk about the development of the plot through the story and discuss possible reasons for developing the book in this way.

Figure 35.1   Plot Profile

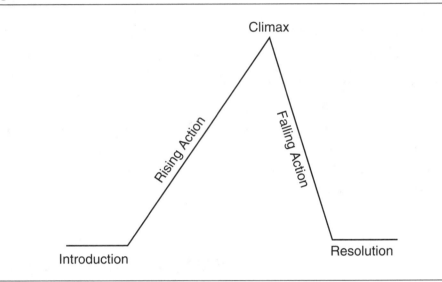

How Else Can We Use This Strategy?

Group Profile: In a group discussion, students express their opinions about the excitement level at the end of each chapter. All suggested levels are then averaged and the average plotted to create a group profile.

Comparison Profile: Students profile two separate books and compare graphs.

Where Can We Learn More?

Johnson, T. D., & Louis, D. R. (1987). *Literacy through literature.* Portsmouth, NH: Heinemann.

McGhee, C. (1998). Plot profiles. *Ideas into action.* Retrieved from http://www .schools.ash.org.au/brcour/plot.htm

Pappas, C. C., Kiefer, B. Z., & Levstik, L. S. (1999). *An integrated language perspective in the elementary school: An action approach* (3rd ed.). New York: Addison Wesley Longman.

Tompkins, G. E. (1998). *Language arts: Content and teaching strategies* (4th ed.). Upper Saddle River, NJ: Prentice Hall.

Tompkins, G. E. (2004). *Fifty literacy strategies: Step by step* (2nd ed.). Upper Saddle River, NJ: Pearson-Prentice Hall.

Figure 35.2   Plot Profile Template

Name _____

Date _____

TITLE OF BOOK: _____

	Chapter 1	Chapter 2	Chapter 3	Chapter 4	Chapter 5	Chapter 6	Chapter 7	Chapter 8	Chapter 9	Chapter 10
Edge of your seat										
Can't put it down										
Moderate										
Calm										
Dull										

Comments:

Ch.1 _____

Ch.2 _____

Ch.3 _____

Ch.4 _____

Ch.5 _____

Ch.6 _____

Ch.7 _____

Ch.8 _____

Ch.9 _____

Ch.10 _____

Copyright © 2006 by Corwin Press. All rights reserved. Reprinted from *60 Strategies for Improving Reading Comprehension in Grades K – 8*, by Kathleen Feeney Jonson. Thousand Oaks, CA: Corwin Press, www.corwinpress.com. Reproduction authorized only for the local school site that has purchased this book.

36

P–M–I Evaluation (Pluses–Minuses –Interesting Aspects)

Suggested Grade Levels: 3 to 8

Elements Addressed: Plot/theme, expository text

Meta-Strategies Incorporated: Making connections, determining important information, summarizing and synthesizing

Supplies: Text with controversial content

WHAT IS P-M-I EVALUATION? ●

P-M-I is an organizational strategy in which students identify the pluses (P's), minuses (M's), and interesting aspects (I's) of an issue. Edward DeBono (1986) is credited with developing the strategy.

When Do We Use It?

This technique works well when students use it to evaluate their own ideas about an issue before reading a piece of literature. Students may also use it to reflect on a piece of literature after reading it.

Why Do We Use It?

P-M-I evaluation requires students to organize their thoughts about an issue before reading or to reflect on an issue after reading. It is a powerful tool for forcing students to evaluate critically.

How Do We Use P-M-I Evaluation?

Before beginning this activity with the class, the teacher selects one or more controversial statements related to a reading. If more than one statement is suggested, students choose one to focus on. They then divide their paper into three columns. The first column they label P (pluses, or positive things about the issue); the second they label M (minuses, or negative things); the third is I (what the students find interesting about the issue). The teacher may suggest that each student come up with a given number of entries under each heading (e.g., five).

After students have completed their evaluation, they share their conclusions.

Figure 36.1

P-M-I Evaluation

Based on a discussion of fighting in the Civil War after a reading assignment from a social studies textbook

PLUS	MINUS	INTERESTING
To end the institution of slavery in the United States. Slavery is immoral and unethical.	Soldiers, young and old, lost their lives in war.	Three million soldiers fought in the Union and Confederate armies.

Contributed by Stephanie Chin, Matt Sullivan, and Paola Caoile, San Francisco, CA, Summer 2004.

Where Can We Learn More?

DeBono, E. (1986). PMI: The treatment of ideas. In *CoRT Thinking*. New York: Pergamon Press.

DeBono, E. (1987). *Letters to thinkers: Further thoughts on lateral thinking.* New York: Penguin Books.

Lazear, D. (1991). *Seven ways of teaching: The artistry of teaching with multiple intelligences.* Palatine, IL: Skylight.

37

Quaker Reading

Also Called: Pop Corn

Suggested Grade Levels: 3 to 8

Elements Addressed: Plot/theme, character, expository text

Meta-Strategies Incorporated: Making connections, monitoring reading for meaning (clarifying)

Supplies: Narrative or expository text, lined paper, pens or pencils

WHAT IS QUAKER READING? ●

Quaker reading is a meeting of students to share responses to a piece of literature as recorded in their journals. Students volunteer at random to read aloud from their writing, just as Quakers speak at random in a meeting. While one person reads, other students listen actively.

When Do We Use It?

This technique is effective after a section of reading and as readers progress through the text.

Why Do We Use It?

This strategy helps students develop the skills of rereading text, skimming, recalling details, locating information, listening carefully and attentively, sequencing, and making decisions. It encourages students to reread and identify a passage that holds special meaning for them. It also validates a student's personal reactions to a work and allows the student to express those reactions in a nonjudgmental setting.

How Do We Use Quaker Reading?

Students select from a piece of literature phrases, sentences, or words that they find particularly meaningful or that create a vivid mental image. They record their selections in the left-hand column of a journal. In the right-hand column, they reflect on why each passage evokes a special meaning or image.

Students then form a large circle. At random, they stand, one at a time, and read aloud from their passages for several minutes. When the reader finishes and sits down, another student stands and begins. Students who are not reading listen actively to the passage being read. Students read their selections whenever they seem to connect to the passage just read; there is no predetermined order.

Teachers should plan to participate with students during this activity. Students may be quiet for long periods of time in the beginning, and the teacher should be prepared to read aloud as an example to the students.

How Else Can We Use This Strategy?

Illustrations: Students illustrate their verbal images in their journals and share the illustrations when they read.

Read-Around: Each student chooses a favorite passage to read aloud and practices it before the group comes together. Students read, one after another. The same passage may be read more than once. Students do not comment on the passages but simply listen. After everyone has shared, the class may discuss overall impressions.

Where Can We Learn More?

Burke, J. (1998). *The English teacher's companion: A complete guide to classroom, curriculum, and the profession.* Portsmouth, NH: Boynton/Cook.

San Francisco Unified School District. (2003). *Sample lesson plan for "between the world and me," by Richard Wright.* Retrieved March 3, 2005, from http://portal.sfusd.edu/data/HR/HS_English_LP.pdf

Tompkins, G. E. (2004). *Fifty literacy strategies: Step by step* (2nd ed.). Upper Saddle River, NJ: Pearson-Prentice Hall.

Question–Ans Relationshi

Suggested Grade Levels: K to 8

Elements Addressed: Plot/theme, character, expository text

Meta-Strategies Incorporated: Asking questions, making inferences

Supplies: Narrative or expository text, handout with questions arranged by category and with room for students to write answers to the questions, pens or pencils

WHAT IS A QUESTION–ANSWER RELATIONSHIP?

Question–answer relationships, or QARs, are questions organized by category depending on where students may find information to answer the questions. Taffy Raphael first developed the strategy in 1982 to teach children how to identify the types of questions asked of them and the appropriate sources of information to answer those questions.

When Do We Use It?

Students answer questions using this strategy after they have finished reading.

Why Do We Use It?

Teachers use question–answer relationships to help students conceptualize and develop comprehension. Through this strategy, students learn to locate information from various sources, combining their personal knowledge with information from the text to find answers. The strategy is especially effective when students are having difficulty finding meaning in what they read. When they become familiar with the types of questions to ask about literature and how to find answers to those questions, they also learn to work more independently.

How Do We Use Question–Answer Relationships?

Before beginning this activity, the teacher determines questions for students to answer after they have read a piece of literature. Questions fall into two umbrella categories, with two subcategories under each umbrella. The categories are as follows:

1. *In the Book.* Students can answer these questions directly from what the author has written.
   (a) *Right There.* Students can find answers within a single sentence.
   (b) *Think and Search (Putting It Together).* Students must draw information from different parts of the book to find answers to these questions.

2. *In My Head.* These questions require students to draw from their personal experience to find the answers.
   (a) *Author and Me.* Students combine what they already know with what the author has written to find the answers. They infer information from evidence provided.
   (b) *On My Own.* Students draw from their personal experience and could answer the questions without ever reading the book.

When introducing this activity, the teacher explains the different categories and gives some examples of each kind of question. Students discuss the answers to sample questions as a group and talk about how they found the answers.

Raphael (1986) suggested that teachers begin by introducing only the two main categories, "In the Book" and "In My Head." Students first have time to analyze responses on those two dimensions only. After they are comfortable with the two main relationships, the teacher can introduce subcategories, beginning with "Right There" and "Think and Search" and then, when students are successful, extending to "Author and Me" and "On My Own." During these introductory question-and-answer discussions, the teacher connects students' answers to the QAR categories. For example, the teacher might comment, "I noticed that you needed to look in several places 'In the Book' to find the answer. That's why it's called a 'Think and Search' and then 'Put It Together.' Good job!"

Later, when students are confident with the QAR activity, the teacher can hand each student a list of questions, organized by category. Students then have an opportunity to work alone or in groups to determine and write down their answers. As an advanced activity, students may write their own questions and answers, dividing them into the same categories.

How Else Can We Use This Strategy?

Two Categories: Younger students work better with questions in only the two main categories: (1) "In the Book" and (2) "In My Head."

Reciprocal Questioning: Students work in pairs, with their books open, creating questions for their partner to answer. The partner answers the question and identifies its QAR category ("In the Book" or "In My Head").

Where Can We Learn More?

Cortese, E. E. (2003). The application of question-answer relationship strategies to pictures. *The Reading Teacher, 57,* 374–380.

Ezell, H. K. (1996). Maintenance and generalization of QAR reading comprehension strategies. *Reading Research and Instruction, 36,* 64–81.

Helfeldt, J. P., & Henk, W. A. (1990). Reciprocal question-and-answer relationships: An instructional technique for at-risk learners. *Journal of Reading, 33.*

McLaughlin, M., & Allen, M. B. (2002). *Guided comprehension: A teaching model for grades 3–8.* Newark: International Reading Association.

Mesmer, H. A. E., & Hutchins, E. J. (2002). Using QAR with charts and graphs. *The Reading Teacher, 56,* 21–25.

Ouzts, D. T. (1998). Enhancing the connection between literature and the social studies using the question–answer relationship. *Social Studies and the Younger Learner, 12*(4), 26–28.

Raphael, T. E. (1982). Question-answering strategies for children. *The Reading Teacher, 36,* 186–191.

Raphael, T. E. (1986). Teaching question answer relationships, revisited. *The Reading Teacher, 39*(6), 515–523.

Figure 38.1

Four Types of Question–Answer Relationships

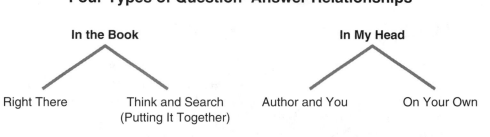

39

Questioning the Author

> Suggested Grade Levels: 3 to 8
>
> Elements Addressed: Plot/theme, expository text
>
> Meta-Strategies Incorporated: Monitoring reading for meaning (clarifying), making connections, determining important information, asking questions, making inferences (predicting)
>
> Supplies: Narrative or expository text

● WHAT IS QUESTIONING THE AUTHOR?

Questioning the author (QTA) is a strategy that forces students to figure out what the author *means,* not just what the author *writes.* The strategy was developed by Isabel Beck, Margaret McKeown, Rebecca Hamilton, and Linda Kucan (1997) to help students get actively engaged with both narrative and expository text, especially text that is dense and difficult for the reader.

When Do We Use It?

Students engage in this strategy throughout the reading process.

Why Do We Use It?

Often students read only the author's words in text. This strategy helps them to construct meaning from what they read by bringing prior knowledge and experience to the author's words. It forces students to look for meaning beyond the author's words.

How Do We Use Questioning the Author?

Before introducing the QTA strategy to students, the teacher selects a text, reads it to find important ideas, and thinks about what difficulties

132

students might have in finding these ideas. Next, the teacher chooses places within the text where the group will stop reading and discuss. Sections should be based on ideas, with stopping points where students should construct meaning; they need not be determined by paragraphs or other divisions within the text. Finally, the teacher writes questions that will force students to think about the content and what it means.

The teacher and students sit in a circle or a horseshoe shape, facing each other. Each has a copy of the book or story to be discussed. The teacher begins by reading the first section aloud. It could be as short as a single sentence. Next, the teacher asks questions. Students will likely begin by answering the questions with information exactly as it is presented in the text. The teacher then asks more questions to encourage students to think more about the text and what it actually means.

Next, the teacher reads aloud a second section of text or asks students to read to themselves and stop at a given point for discussion. The teacher then asks the next question or questions to get students to think about that part.

While doing QTAs, teachers point out to students that authors are not perfect. Authors don't always write clearly; they sometimes assume students know more than they actually know, and they sometimes leave out important pieces of information. Through the QTA strategy, students learn to figure out what the author means, not just to memorize what is written.

Where Can We Learn More?

Beck, I., McKeown, M., Hamilton, R., & Kucan, L. (1997). *Questioning the author: An approach to enhancing student engagement with text.* Newark, DE: International Reading Association.

Beck, I., McKeown, M., Sandora, C., & Kucan, L. (1996). Questioning the author: A yearlong classroom implementation to engage students with text. *The Elementary School Journal 96,* 385–414.

Figure 39.1

Questioning the Author (QtA)

QtA is an excellent way to get students engaged in both narrative and expository text, especially if they are having difficulty comprehending what they read. Beck et al., who developed the QtA strategy in 1996, recommend using three different types of queries: initiating, follow-up, and narrative. Questions are very important in the implementation of QtA because they link text with meaning and are the driving force in helping students construct meaning.

Initiating Questions:

- **What is the author trying to say here?**

- **What is the author's message?**

- **What is the author talking about?**

(Continued)

Figure 39.1 (Continued)

Follow-up Questions:

To help students think about the ideas and thoughts behind the actual words of the author:

- **What does the author mean here?**

- **Does the author explain this clearly?**

To help students connect ideas previously learned with the text and to connect ideas previously read in the text:

- **Does this make sense with what the author told us before?**

- **How does this connect to what the author told us before?**

To help students figure out the author's reasons for including certain information in the text:

- **Does the author tell us why?**

- **Why do you think the author tells us this now?**

Narrative Questions (for fiction only):

To help students think about characters and their motivations:

- **How do things look for this character now?**

- **Given what the author has already told us about this character, what do you think he's up to?**

To help students think about plot and how the author has crafted it:

- **How does the author let you know that something has changed?**

- **How has the author settled this for us?**

40

Quickwriting

Also Called: Freewriting

Suggested Grade Levels: K to 8

Elements Addressed: Plot/theme, character, expository text

Meta-Strategies Incorporated: Making connections, summarizing and synthesizing

Supplies: Narrative or expository text, lined paper, pens or pencils

WHAT IS QUICKWRITING?

Quickwriting is a short activity in which students respond to a piece of literature in writing for five to ten minutes. Students do not organize their thoughts but simply write what comes to mind about a specific topic. The emphasis is on content rather than on mechanics.

When Do We Use It?

This strategy can be used before, during, or after reading a piece of literature. When used before reading, students explore their own ideas about an issue related to an upcoming reading. During or after reading, students think and write about issues in the piece of literature.

Why Do We Use It?

Quickwriting helps students discover what they already know about a topic or a piece of literature. Without worrying about the mechanics of writing, they are able to develop insight into their own thinking; they discover, explore, and develop ideas. Through quickwriting, students also expand their writing ability.

How Do We Use Quickwriting?

The teacher gives students a topic and tells them to write continuously about that topic for some specific amount of time, usually five to ten minutes.

Students are instructed to write without stopping, keeping their pencil moving the entire time. They should put as many ideas as possible on the paper; they may reflect on the reading, make connections, and/or draw from personal experience as they write. Students who cannot think of anything more to write before the time has ended should rewrite their last sentence repeatedly until a new thought comes to mind.

Students are instructed not to worry about spelling, punctuation, or grammar. After they put words on paper, they do not revise the words but continue writing new thoughts.

How Else Can We Use This Strategy?

Discussion: A discussion based on ideas generated through quickwriting enables students to share their knowledge and build on what they know. Students may complete a second quickwrite after hearing what their classmates have to say.

Quickdraw: Students draw pictures, following the same guidelines: They generate as many ideas as possible without revising their work. This variation works especially well with young readers and with English language learners.

Follow-Up: Students circle a key concept or idea in their quickwrite and later develop a finished piece of writing based on that idea.

Where Can We Learn More?

King, D. (1983). Teaching persona through freewriting. *Exercise Exchange, 28,* 2–21.

Knox-Quinn, C. (1993). David Bohm's dialogue, the freewrite dance, and "aspects." *Writing Notebook: Visions for Learning, 10,* 4–6.

Rief, L. (2002). Quick-writes: Leads to literacy. *Voices from the Middle, 10*(1), 50–51.

Tompkins, G. E. (2002). *Language arts: Content and teaching strategies* (5th ed.). Upper Saddle River, NJ: Prentice Hall.

Tompkins, G. E. (2004). *Fifty literacy strategies: Step by step* (2nd ed.). Upper Saddle River, NJ: Pearson-Prentice Hall.

Wilhelm, J. D, Baker, T. N., & Dube, J. (2001). *Strategic reading: Guiding students to lifelong literacy.* Portsmouth, NH: Boynton/Cook.

Figure 40.1

Quickwrite

Based on the Book *If I Only Had a Horn*

Louis Armstrong sounds like an amazing man. He *really* loved Jazz music. It was hard if you were growing up in New Orleans like he did in early 1900. It was very different from today. I think it's so sad that Louis Armstrong had a tough life. Sometimes his family didn't have enough food to eat. I feel very lucky after reading about Louis Armstrong when he was a kid.

Book used: Orgill, R. (1997). *If I only had a horn: Young Louis Armstrong.* Boston: Houghton Mifflin.

Contributed by Stephanie Abramowitz, San Francisco, CA, Fall 2003.

Figure 40.2

Quickwrite

With Guided Imagery

Based on the Short Story "A Prospect of the Sea"

It is high summer, and you are lying in a corn field. You are feeling happy because you have no work to do and the weather is hot. You can hear the corn sway from side to side beside you. The noise of birds, whistling from the branches of the trees that hide the house vibrate within you. Lying flat on your back you stare up into the unbroken blue sky falling over the edge of the corn. The wind, after the warm rain before noon, smells of rabbits and cattle. You stretch yourself like a cat and put your arms behind your back. Now you are riding on the sea, swimming through the golden corn waves, gliding along the heavens like a bird. Now you are in giant sized boots, springing over the fields. You rise to your feet and wander out of the corn to the strip of river by the hillside. You put your fingers in the water, making mock sea waves to roll the stones over and shake the weeds. You make up a story as the fish swim past. It tells of a drowned princess . . .

After reading this passage aloud, instruct students: Begin to write. Do not stop to think. Just write about where you are and what happens next.

Story Used: Thomas, D. (1966). *A Prospect of the sea and other stories and prose writings.* Aldine. Retrieved from http://www.dailywriting.net/guided-imagery.htm

Contributed by Lindsay Kahn and Kristina Reguero, San Francisco, CA, Summer 2004.

41

Readers' Theater

Suggested Grade Levels: 3 to 8

Elements Addressed: Plot/theme, character

Meta-Strategies Incorporated: Making connections, visualizing, making inferences

Supplies: Text with a strong plot, a lot of dialogue, and several characters; name tags or simple objects to distinguish characters

● WHAT IS READERS' THEATER?

Readers' theater is a student performance of a script; it is similar to a radio play. Students read from an original script, using their voices and expressions to act out the scenes.

When Do We Use It?

This strategy is most effective when used after students first read a text.

Why Do We Use It?

Students practice writing, reading, and performing. They interpret a text, create dialogue, and become the characters that they portray. The activity also helps students to increase fluency and comprehension. It encourages collaborative group work. When students see their peers' performance, their appreciation for the literature often grows.

How Do We Use Readers' Theater?

A piece of literature is selected for use; it can be a published book, a song, a poem, or a folktale. The teacher writes a script for one scene as a sample to be discussed before students write their own scenes. Students and the teacher discuss the use of dialogue to convey the story and the use of a narrator for parts that are not presented as dialogue.

The rest of the piece of literature is divided among individual students or among small groups of students working together. Students are reminded to use a narrator in their work as they create a script for their section. After all of the parts are written, they are combined as one script.

When the script is ready, students select parts to perform. They practice reading aloud, dramatically and fluently, using their voices, gestures, and facial expressions to convey their interpretation of the material. Students may use name tags, simple props, or small articles (such as a hat) as a costume to indicate a particular character. They may stand or sit as they read. The performance is similar to a radio play and does not involve acting or memorization. No scenery or stage is used.

How Else Can We Use This Strategy?

Group Script: Students create a script as a group project.

Prepared Script: Younger students use a prepared script.

Original Stories: Older students write their own stories and create scripts from these original works.

History Re-Creation: Students act out scenes—especially historical events—from textbooks.

Where Can We Learn More?

Busching, B. A. (1981). Readers theatre: An education for language and life. *Language Arts, 58*(3): 330–338.

Rasinski, T., & Padak, N. (2001). *From phonics to fluency.* New York: Longman.

Rasinski, T., & Padak, N. (2004). *Effective reading strategies: Teaching children who find reading difficult* (3rd ed.). Upper Saddle River, NJ: Prentice Hall.

Wilhelm, J. D. (1998). Learning by being: Drama as total immersion. *Voices from the Middle, 6*(2) (December), 3–10.

Figure 41.1   Step-by-Step Instructions for Readers' Theater

READERS' THEATER STEP BY STEP

Step 1: Reading the Selection

The selection is read and discussed. Prereading preparation includes activating schema, building background and vocabulary to be used during the reading, and setting a purpose for reading.

> Although no stage or props are required in readers' theater, participants might sit on stools. Pantamiming and gestures are used when appropriate but should be used sparingly.

Step 2: Preparing the Script

After the selection has been discussed in much the same way as it would be in a directed reading activity, students who will reenact the piece reread the play and discuss the characters and may create a character map. The teacher can let students decide who will take which parts or assign parts herself. If the group has both high- and low-achieving readers, the teacher might choose parts for the low-achieving reader that involve less reading and are easier to read.

> Pieces that work best for readers' theater are those that have a great deal of dialog and a minimum of narration. Stories, poems, chapter books, and even historical biographies can be portrayed through readers' theater. For long works, it might be best to portray excerpts of key portions of the text.

Step 3: Interpreting the Script

Once the script has been prepared, students discuss how they will portray each character: what facial expressions they will use, what gestures they will employ, and how they will use their voices to convey emotions.

The script may be written by the teacher or the group. Group writing is preferable, but guidance might be required. The group discusses how they want to rewrite the script. Dialog from the selection should remain intact. Narrative segments from the selection might be summarized, especially if they are lengthy. Or they may be translated into dialog. Additional narration may need to be composed for sake of clarity.

Students can highlight their dialog with markers. Narrations can be underlined. Narrator's lines can be added as needed to introduce scenes, provide transitions, or summarize events.

> There are a number of ready-made scripts for readers' theater. Check the Internet and teachers' supply stores.

Step 4: Practicing

Students practice reading their scripts. At the end of each reading, they discuss things that each did well and what might be done to improve the performance or the script.

Step 5: Performing

The script is performed for the class.

Figure 41.2

READERS' THEATER

This example shows the original text and the script that was prepared from it. The text is taken from *Flying Solo* by Ralph Fletcher.

CHAPTER 4
7:19 A.M.
Mrs. Muchmore

Wendy Muchmore woke up with a throbbing headache. Every bone in her body ached; every joint was on fire. She wanted to go back to sleep, but she couldn't. Today she as subbing in Mr. Fabiano's sixth-grade class at the Paulson Elementary School. She had to be there by 8:12 a.m. sharp.

She tried to sit up, but lifting her head brought on such a fit of dizziness that she felt like throwing up. She groaned. There was no choice but to call in and take a sick day. They would have to find a substitute for the substitute. With some effort, she lifted the heavy phone book and found the number of the school.

"Paulson Elementary School."

"Yes, good morning, this is Mrs. Muchmore." Her voice sounded shaky. "I am scheduled to substitute for Mr. Fabiano today, sixth grade. Unfortunately I'm sick today so I can't come in. I'm so—"

"You're supposed to call the Registry when you're sick." It was Mrs. Pierce, the school secretary, and she sounded annoyed. "That's district policy. Didn't they tell you that?"

"Yes, well, I forgot—"

"I'll make a note of it," Mrs. Pierce said, "but next time please phone the Registry." She hung up. Wendy sighed and put down phone.

Scene 4
7:19 A.M.
Mrs. Muchmore

Characters:
Mrs. Muchmore, the substitute
Mrs. Muchmore's husband
Mrs. Pierce, the school secretary
Narrator

Narrator: Wendy Muchmore woke up with a start.

Husband: Wendy, what's wrong? You don't look like you feel well!

Mrs. Muchmore: Ugh. Every bone in my body aches. My head is throbbing and my joints are on fire!

Husband: You had better go back to bed.

Mrs. Muchmore: I can't. I have to sub in Mr. Fabiano's sixth grade class and I have to be there by 8:12 A.M. sharp!

Narrator: Mrs. Muchmore groans and falls back on the pillow, a wave of dizziness washing over her.

Husband: You can't go in. You are too sick. They will just have to find a substitute for the substitute!

Narrator: Wendy Muchmore nods, and with much effort, lifts up the heavy phone book and finds the number of the school. . . . RING RING!

Mrs. Pierce: Paulson Elementary School.

Mrs. Muchmore (shakily): Yes, good morning, this is Mrs. Muchmore. I'm scheduled to substitute for Mr. Fabiano today, sixth grade. Unfortunately I'm sick today so I can't come in. I'm so—

Mrs. Pierce (annoyed): You're supposed to call the Registry when you're sick. That's district policy. Didn't they tell you that?

Mrs. Muchmore: Yes, well, I forgot—

Mrs. Pierce: I'll make a note of it, but next time please phone the Registry.

Narrator: Mrs. Muchmore sighs and puts down the phone.

Book used: Fletcher, R. (1998). *Flying solo*. New York: Dell Yearling, Random House.

Contributed by Kate Working, San Francisco, CA, Fall 2003.

42

Read-Pair-Share

Suggested Grade Levels: 3 to 8

Elements Addressed: Plot/theme, character, expository text

Meta-Strategies Incorporated: Asking questions, summarizing and synthesizing

Supplies: Narrative or expository text, summary forms (one for each student), pens or pencils

• WHAT IS READ-PAIR-SHARE?

Read-pair-share is a strategy that involves partner reading and questioning. Partners question each other about a selection they have just read, asking *who*, *what*, *where*, *when*, *why*, and *how*. During some read-pair-shares, the teacher provides a summary sheet for the listener to record what the partner shared about the text.

When Do We Use It?

This strategy is used after the reading of a text.

Why Do We Use It?

Read-pair-share helps students recall and clarify text as they are reading, or after they have completed a selection. Struggling readers may benefit when paired with stronger readers who can help give them access to text otherwise beyond their understanding.

How Do We Use the Read-Pair-Share Strategy?

Before students begin reading, the teacher leads a discussion about *who*, *what*, *where*, *when*, *why*, and *how* questions, describing the different issues addressed by each. The teacher may wish to model the procedure by orally sharing the main points in a story recently read aloud, while students make notes on the record form. The teacher could leave out important information as he or she recaps the text so that students realize that their partners may miss significant details as they share what they have read.

Students choose or are assigned partners. Two struggling readers should not be paired together. Next, they are instructed to open their books to a particular passage and to read the selection silently. After reading, one partner shares the main points in the passage. The listener responds to the review, offering suggestions for elaboration. Then the other partner has a turn using a different passage. Once this partner has finished sharing, the listener provides feedback. Whenever partners cannot remember the *who, what, where, when, why,* or *how,* they look together at the reading selection to find the answers.

How Else Can We Use This Strategy?

Think-Pair-Share: Students listen to a question, think about it, and pair up with a partner to discuss their thoughts. The three-step process provides "think time" for review and rehearsal before "sharing" what they know with a partner. It is a useful strategy for review of what has been learned at the end of a lesson. At the close of the activity, students share their partners' thoughts with the entire group.

Mapping your partner's responses: In this variation of read-pair-share, the listener creates a map of the partner's responses to the *who, what where,* and *when* questions. To create the map, the listener draws a circle in the middle of a piece of paper and writes the name of the story in the circle. Then the student draws four lines radiating from the circle and labels each line "who," "what," "where," and "when." As the partner tells specific details from the story, the listener notes each on the proper "spoke." At the end of the activity, students share their maps with others in the class.

Where Can We Learn More?

Blachowicz, C., & Ogle, D. (2001). *Reading comprehension: Strategies for independent learners.* New York: Guilford Press.

Herrell, A., & Jordan, M. (2002). *Fifty active learning strategies for improving reading comprehension.* Upper Saddle River, NJ: Merrill Prentice Hall.

Figure 42.1

Read-Pair-Share

SUMMARY SHEET

Name of Sharing Partner: _____

Name of Listening Partner: _____

Date: _____

Title of Book: _____

_____ Where does the story take place?

_____ When does the story take place?

_____ How does the story begin?

_____ Who are the main characters?

    _____ Partner gives names of characters

    _____ Partner gives number of characters

    _____ Partner tells whether characters are male, female, animals, etc.

_____ What was the problem in the story?

    _____ Partner tells the main character's primary goal

_____ What happened in the story?

    _____ Partner tells the main events in order (beginning, middle, and end)

_____ How was the problem solved?

    _____ Partner explains how the story ends.

Copyright © 2006 by Corwin Press. All rights reserved. Reprinted from *60 Strategies for Improving Reading Comprehension in Grades K – 8*, by Kathleen Feeney Jonson. Thousand Oaks, CA: Corwin Press, www.corwinpress. com. Reproduction authorized only for the local school site that has purchased this book.

Figure 42.2 Sample Map of Read-Share-Pair Responses

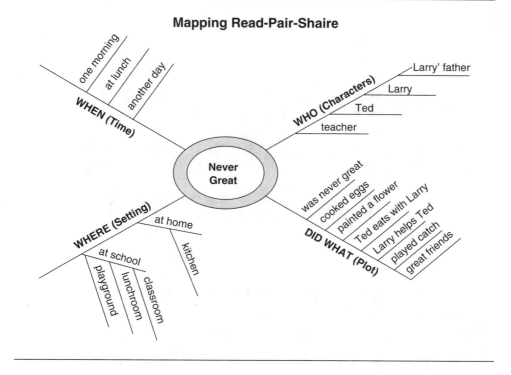

Mapping Read-Pair-Shaire

WHEN (Time): one morning, at lunch, another day

WHO (Characters): Larry' father, Larry, Ted, teacher

Never Great

WHERE (Setting): at home, kitchen, at school, classroom, lunchroom, playground

DID WHAT (Plot): was never great, cooked eggs, painted a flower, Ted eats with Larry, Larry helps Ted, played catch, great friends

43

Reciprocal Questioning (ReQuest)

Suggested Grade Levels: 3 to 8

Elements Addressed: Plot/theme, expository text

Meta-Strategies Incorporated: Monitoring reading for meaning (clarifying), asking questions, making inferences (predicting), summarizing and synthesizing

Supplies: Narrative or expository text

● WHAT IS RECIPROCAL QUESTIONING?

Reciprocal questioning, or ReQuest, is a structure outlined by Anthony Manzo in 1969 for conducting comprehension lessons. In this cooperative strategy, teachers and students exchange the roles of asking and answering questions about the text.

When Do We Use It?

This strategy is used throughout the reading of text, fiction or nonfiction.

Why Do We Use It?

When they engage in reciprocal questioning, students use questioning, clarification, inference, and prediction to improve their comprehension of text. The strategy requires careful and deliberate reading of the text, both for the student creating a question and for those answering. ReQuest helps students learn how to compose and answer questions about text through active observation and participation. The strategy also teaches students to work together.

How Do We Use Reciprocal Questioning?

Before this activity begins, the teacher divides the text into sections. These sections may be only as long as a sentence, or they may include one or more paragraphs, depending on the complexity of the material.

To introduce the activity, teacher and students read the first assigned portion of a text silently. Both the teacher and the students close the book after reading. Then the students ask the teacher questions about the text, and the teacher models how to answer questions clearly and accurately. Students may ask any of the following:

- Questions about the meaning of particular words
- Questions that can be answered directly from the text
- Questions that require drawing on common knowledge about the world
- Questions that relate the text to personal lives
- Questions that encourage thinking beyond the text
- Questions that require finding information outside of the text

Next, teacher and students reverse roles. Participants read the next part of the text and then close their books. Then the students try to answer the questions asked by the teacher.

After this introduction to questioning, students are divided into small groups. They may now work together in teams, taking turns asking and answering questions. Students read the next section of text silently. Then one student in each group asks a question of other group members.

The same student who asked the question clarifies any part of the text that other students had difficulty understanding. When students have read enough to make a prediction about the rest of the book, the questioner can ask students to predict what might happen in the next section and then verify it in the text.

Members of the group read the next section of text silently, and then a second student takes a turn as group leader, repeating the steps followed for the first section (question, clarification, and prediction). The process continues, with each student taking a turn as leader.

How Else Can We Use This Strategy?

Questioning the Teacher: Students ask questions of the teacher, who attempts to answer them as completely as possible.

Where Can We Learn More?

Herrell, A., & Jordan, M. (2002). *Fifty active learning strategies for improving reading comprehension.* Upper Saddle River, NJ: Merrill Prentice Hall.

Manzo, A. V. (1969). The request procedure. *The Journal of Reading, 13,* 123–126.

Palincsar, A. S., & Brown, A. L. (1986). Interactive teaching to promote independent learning from text. *The Reading Teacher, 39,* 771–777.

Tompkins, G. E. (2004). *Fifty literacy strategies: Step by step* (2nd ed.). Upper Saddle River, NJ: Pearson-Prentice Hall.

Figure 43.1

ReQuest Questions
for a Unit on Folktales, Myths, and Fairy Tales

The following are questions a teacher used to introduce and model a ReQuest lesson. The teacher's goal was to help students determine the genre of a piece of literature. The teacher invited the students to also ask questions.

Teacher and students each read silently the first section, then close their books.

Teacher's Question: Does the story take place in the past, the present, or the future?

Student Question: Do the characters wear old-fashioned-looking clothes?

Student Question: Does the story begin with, "Once upon a time. . . . "?

Teacher and students each read silently the next section, then close their books.

Teacher's Question: Is the story true?

Student Question: Are the characters in the story humans?

Student Question: Do animals talk in the story?

Teacher and students each read silently the next section, then close their books.

Teacher's Question: Is there some sort of magic in the story?

Student Question: Does somebody disappear?

Teacher and students each read silently to the end of the story, then close their books.

Teacher's Question: Does the story have a moral?

Student Question: What's the message you're supposed to get from this story?

Student Question: Is this story telling us how to act or not act?

Teacher's Question: Is this story a fable, folktale, myth, or fairy tale?

Student Question: Does the story explain why certain things happen?

44

Response Log

Also called: Literature Response Journal

Suggested Grade Levels: 3 to 8

Elements Addressed: Plot/theme, character, expository text

Meta-Strategies Incorporated: Making connections, summarizing and synthesizing

Supplies: Narrative text, lined paper, pens or pencils

WHAT IS A RESPONSE LOG? ●

A response log is a place for students to write their reactions to literature. The writing is informal, conveying the reader's experiences, ideas, feelings, and other responses to the reading. Reading response logs are open-ended invitations to students to register their feelings about a book in writing, drawing, or both.

When Do We Use It?

Students write in a response log throughout the reading process.

Why Do We Use It?

Keeping a response log forces students to reflect about the text, helps them make personal connections to the text, and encourages them to use analytical skills. The log honors individual response and gives students an opportunity to reflect on themselves as readers. The strategy also allows teachers to evaluate the needs of individual students.

How Do We Use Response Logs?

Students keep running journals as they read; they may choose to organize their logs or to use the log for quickwriting. Students select passages to write about and/or record questions related to the literature. They may write notes to summarize what they have read but should move beyond that to record how their ideas change as they read. Students may write about personal experiences brought to mind by the story or compare people they know and stories from their past to those in the literature. They may describe characters in detail or record their opinions about the behaviors of the characters. Finally, they may predict what will happen next in the story.

Initial attempts of students in the younger grades may be limited to one-line entries. As these students gain experience responding to literature in their logs, however, their responses become more detailed, beyond literal retellings.

How Else Can We Use This Strategy?

Directed Response: Instead of giving students time to write freely, the teacher prompts students to write about something specific. For example, the teacher might tell students,

- Imagine you are a character in the book. Tell what you might have done.
- Give a character some advice.
- Pretend you are a character and write a journal entry expressing that character's feelings about some event in the story.
- Write about something you liked (or disliked) in the story, and tell why.
- Write about what you wish had happened.
- Write about your feelings as you read.
- Write about some vocabulary that you learned as a result of reading.

The teacher may instead write the beginning of a sentence on the board and ask students to complete the sentence and elaborate on it. Openers might be, for example, "When this happens to me, I feel . . ." or "I wish . . ."

Where Can We Learn More?

Cox, C., & Many, J. (1992). Toward an understanding of the aesthetic response to literature. *Language Arts, 69* (January), 28–33.

Hennings, D. (2002). Literature Response Journals. In *Communication in Action: Teaching Literature-Based Language Arts* (pp. 135–138). New York: Houghton-Mifflin.

Kelly, P. (1990). Guiding young students response to literature. *The Reading Teacher, 43* (March), 464–470.

Figure 44.1 Sample Prompts for Younger Students

Response Log Starters

I liked _____ because . . .

I noticed . . .

I wonder . . .

I felt _____ because . . .

I think . . .

This story makes me think of . . .

I wish . . .

If I were _____, I would . . .

When I . . .

I was surprised by . . .

Copyright © 2006 by Corwin Press. All rights reserved. Reprinted from *60 Strategies for Improving Reading Comprehension in Grades K – 8*, by Kathleen Feeney Jonson. Thousand Oaks, CA: Corwin Press, www.corwinpress. com. Reproduction authorized only for the local school site that has purchased this book.

Figure 44.2 Sample Prompts for Older Students

Response Log Starters

Now I understand...

What impressed me in this chapter (book) . . .

This (character/story) reminded me of . . .

In my opinion . . .

When this happens to me, I feel . . .

One time I . . .

It was (was not) fair when . . .

I think (character/part in the story) is (is not) believable because . . .

The author could have . . .

Why did the author . . .

I think the author was trying to say . . .

If I were _____, I would have . . .

The story (character) is like . . .

To me, the most important part of the book was _____ because . . .

I would like (would not like) _____ to happen to me because . . .

Copyright © 2006 by Corwin Press. All rights reserved. Reprinted from *60 Strategies for Improving Reading Comprehension in Grades K – 8*, by Kathleen Feeney Jonson. Thousand Oaks, CA: Corwin Press, www.corwinpress. com. Reproduction authorized only for the local school site that has purchased this book.

Figure 44.3 Sample Teacher-Directed Reflection

Response Log Starters

Based on Chapter 1 of *The Stories Julian Tells*

Teacher writes on board:

"Choose <u>one</u> to do in your Reading Log-"

"What do you think Julian and Huey's dad will do to them after they ate all the pudding?"

"Have you ever felt as scared as Julian and Huey were as they hid under the bed? Explain why and when."

"Draw a picture of 'a raft of lemons'."

Book used: Cameron, A. (1981). *The stories Julian tells.* New York: Dell Yearling, Random House.

Contributed by Stephanie Abramowitz, San Francisco, CA, Fall 2003.

Semantic Mapping

Suggested Grade Levels: K to 8

Elements Addressed: Plot/theme, expository text

Meta-Strategies Incorporated: Monitoring reading for meaning (clarifying), making inferences (predicting)

Supplies: Narrative or expository text, board or flipchart, and dark-colored marker

● WHAT IS SEMANTIC MAPPING?

Semantic mapping is a strategy for categorizing information and depicting it graphically.

When Do We Use It?

Students use semantic mapping to organize their knowledge about a topic before they begin to read. They may discuss the map again and add to it after they complete their reading.

Why Do We Use It?

This strategy helps students organize and integrate information. Teachers can introduce key concepts and vocabulary before reading begins. Students better understand and remember what they read after first mapping-related information.

The class may revisit the semantic map after students finish reading. At this time, students may add new ideas and concepts. This part of the strategy helps students to recall, organize, and represent important information from their reading. See Figure 45.2 for an example of a map begun prior to reading an expository text and completed after reading.

How Do We Use Semantic Mapping?

The teacher chooses a term that is central to the reading selection, writes it in the middle of the board or on a sheet of a flipchart, and circles it. Next, categories are noted around the central theme, circled, and connected to the main idea with a line. For example, if the reading selection is a book is about a school, the teacher might suggest the categories of people, subjects, and facilities. After this, the teacher asks students to suggest examples for each category and lists the examples in the appropriate place. Finally, the teacher leads a discussion about the terms and how they relate to each other. The map is posted in the room so that students may refer to it as they read and may add new examples if they wish.

How Else Can We Use This Strategy?

Student Brainstorming: The teacher suggests only the central idea and then has the students suggest related terms. After several ideas have been recorded, the students organize their ideas into categories and label the categories.

Where Can We Learn More?

Bromley, K., Irwin-DeVitis, L., & Modlo, M. (1995). *Graphic organizers: Visual strategies for active learning.* New York: Scholastic.

Johnson, D., Pittelman, S., & Heimlich, J. (1986). Semantic mapping. *The Reading Teacher, 39,* 778–783.

McLaughlin, M., & Allen, M. B. (2002). *Guided comprehension: A teaching model for grades 3–8.* Newark, DE: International Reading Association.

Stahl, S., & Vancil, S. (1986). Discussion is what makes semantic maps work. *The Reading Teacher, 40,* 62–67.

Yopp, R. H., & Yopp, H. K. (2001). *Literature-based reading activities* (3rd ed.). Boston: Allyn & Bacon.

Figure 45.1

Semantic Mapping

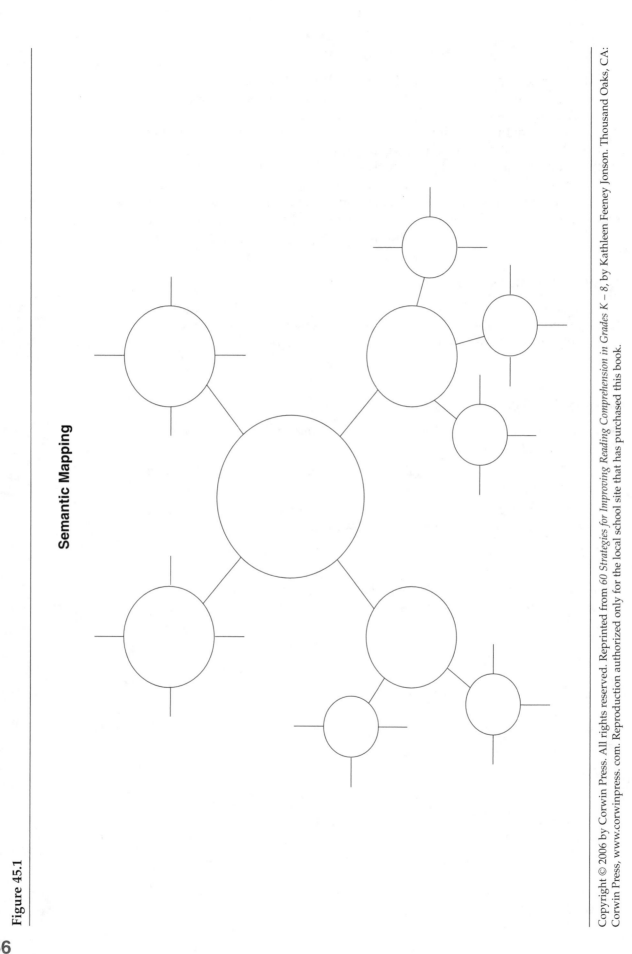

Copyright © 2006 by Corwin Press. All rights reserved. Reprinted from *60 Strategies for Improving Reading Comprehension in Grades K – 8*, by Kathleen Feeney Jonson. Thousand Oaks, CA: Corwin Press, www.corwinpress. com. Reproduction authorized only for the local school site that has purchased this book.

Figure 45.2

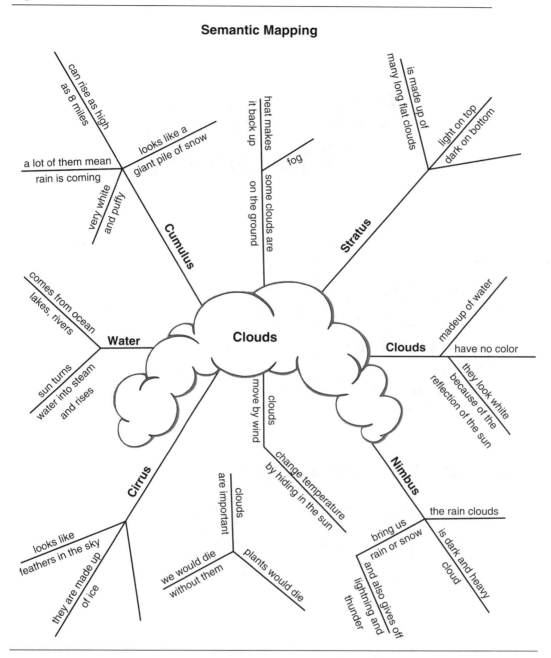

Semantic Mapping

Clouds

Cumulus
- can rise as high as 8 miles
- looks like a giant pile of snow
- a lot of them mean rain is coming
- very white and puffy

Water
- comes from ocean lakes, rivers
- sun turns water into steam and rises

Stratus
- heat makes it back up
- fog
- some clouds are on the ground

- is made up of many long flat clouds
- light on top dark on bottom

Clouds
- madeup of water
- have no color
- they look white because of the reflection of the sun

Cirrus
- looks like feathers in the sky
- they are made up of ice

- clouds move by wind
- change temperature by hiding in the sun
- clouds are important
- we would die without them
- plants would die

Nimbus
- the rain clouds
- bring us rain or snow and also gives off lightning and thunder
- is dark and heavy cloud

46

Sketch-to-Stretch

> Also Called: Visualization
>
> Suggested Grade Levels: K to 5
>
> Elements Addressed: Plot/theme, character
>
> Meta-Strategies Incorporated: Visualizing, summarizing and synthesizing
>
> Supplies: Narrative or expository text; construction paper or poster paper; colored pencils, crayons, or markers

● WHAT IS SKETCH-TO-STRETCH?

Sketch-to-stretch is a strategy that draws on the artistic abilities of students as they interpret literature. Students use sketches and, sometimes, brief text descriptions or notes to express their thoughts about what they have read.

When Do We Use It?

Sketch-to-stretch can be used during or after reading.

Why Do We Use It?

Sketch-to-stretch forces students to recall the main ideas of a story and helps them to understand what they have read. It is a good exercise for visual learners who are better able to express themselves through art than through words. It is also a good activity for students who are English language learners, for beginning readers, or for students who struggle with reading but who can bring the literature to life through pictures. The exercise may help to build the self-confidence of struggling readers and may encourage readers to be creative when responding to text.

How Do We Use Sketch-to-Stretch?

Students read any piece of text, either to themselves or aloud; younger students may listen as the teacher reads. After the reading is done, the teacher leads a discussion about themes in the story and ways to symbolize meaning through illustration. The class talks about possible ways to represent visually what the story means.

The teacher provides a variety of art materials: poster paper, construction paper, markers, colored pencils, and/or crayons. Students are instructed to choose one aspect of the text and draw what it means to them. They may choose a scene, an event, or a character, for example. The teacher tells them to be creative and reminds them that there are many different ways to represent personal meaning; there is no right or wrong sketch or correct interpretation. Students need not limit their artwork to a favorite character or plot but should depict what the story means to them. They may use symbols, images, pictures, lines, shapes, and colors to express their interpretations and feelings. If they like, they may write a quotation or phrase from the book on the paper, invent a title, or describe their work in writing.

After drawing, students discuss their illustrations and what they mean. Following this discussion, students may add to their drawings.

The teacher may collect all drawings and bind them into a class book.

How Else Can We Use This Strategy?

Thought Balloons: Students write thoughts for any characters they draw.

Visual Editor: Students work in pairs to create illustrations for the book.

Journal Sketch: Students make quick sketches in their journals to reflect their feelings.

Where Can We Learn More?

Fountas, I. C., & Pinnel, G. S. (2001). *Guiding readers and writers, grades 3–6.* Portsmouth, NH: Heinemann.

McLaughlin, M., & Allen, M. B. (2002). *Guided comprehension: A teaching model for grades 3–8.* Newark, DE: International Reading Association.

Rasinski, T., & Padak, N. (2004). *Effective reading strategies: Teaching children who find reading difficult* (3rd ed.). Upper Saddle River, NJ: Prentice Hall.

Short, K. G., & Harste, J. C. (1996). *Creating classrooms for authors and inquirers.* Portsmouth, NH: Heinemann.

Short, K., Kauffman, G., & Kahn, L. (2000). "I just *need* to draw": Responding to literature across multiple sign systems. *The Reading Teacher, 54*(October), 160–171.

White, P. E. (1996). Exploring visual response to literature. *Research in the teaching of English, 30,* 114–140.

Whitin, P. E. (1994). Opening potential: Visual response to literature. *Language Arts, 7*(2), 101–107.

Whitin, P. E. (1996). *Sketching stories, stretching minds.* Portsmouth, NH: Heinemann.

Whitin, P. E. (2002). Leading into literature circles through the sketch-to-stretch strategy. *The Reading Teacher, 55,* 444–450.

Figure 46.1

Name: _____ Date: _____

Sketch to Stretch

What did you think of the story? Make a sketch here to show what you think.

Tell what is happening in your sketch. What in the story made you think about this?

_____

_____

_____

Copyright © 2006 by Corwin Press. All rights reserved. Reprinted from *60 Strategies for Improving Reading Comprehension in Grades K – 8*, by Kathleen Feeney Jonson. Thousand Oaks, CA: Corwin Press, www.corwinpress. com. Reproduction authorized only for the local school site that has purchased this book.

Figure 46.2

Jimmy Jet turns into his T.V. set.

Book used: Silverstein, S. (2004, 30th Anniversary edition). *Where the sidewalk ends*. New York: HarperCollins.
Contributed by Julie Walton, San Francisco, CA, Fall 2003.

Figure 46.3

The Brand New Kid by Katie Couric

"...about Lazlo and how he felt different and strange..."

"... he asked with a smile, a look that hadn't been on his face in a while"

Book used: Couric, K. (2000). *The brand new kid*. New York: Scholastic, Inc.
Contributed by Michelle Dong, San Francisco, CA, Fall 2003.

47

SQ3R (Survey-Question-Read-Recite-Review)

Suggested Grade Levels: 6 to 8

Elements Addressed: Expository text

Meta-Strategies Incorporated: Asking questions, making inferences (predicting), summarizing, and synthesizing

Supplies: Expository text; lined paper, pens or pencils

● WHAT IS THE SQ3R STUDY STRATEGY?

SQ3R stands for survey, question, read, recite, and review. The strategy is used to help students learn and remember information in a content area.

When Do We Use It?

Students begin this strategy before they read. They make predictions based on a survey of the literature—titles, subtitles, illustrations, introductions and conclusions, and so on—and write questions they would like answered.

Next, they continue the strategy as they read, looking for answers to their own questions. After they have finished reading, they recite their answers and then review what they have learned.

Why Do We Use It?

The SQ3R strategy helps students learn and remember information. Students are able to focus when reading as they search for the answers to their own questions. Throughout the strategy, they determine what they want to learn, comprehend ideas, and fix what they have learned in memory.

How Do We Use the SQ3R Strategy?

This strategy is carried out in five steps. Because it can be very effective for learning, students should have plenty of opportunities to practice it.

Step 1: Survey. Before they begin reading, students survey (or preview) the literature, reading titles and subheadings, looking at pictures, and skimming the introductions and conclusions. In so doing, they pick out important ideas, activate prior knowledge, and make predictions about what they will read.

Step 2: Question. Students create a question based on each heading. Doing this helps them establish a purpose for reading: to find answers.

Step 3: Read. Students read actively to find the answers to their own questions.

Step 4: Recite. After they have finished reading, students recite from memory—orally or in writing—the answers to their questions and other important information. If they are unable to recite from memory, they reread the material.

Step 5: Review. In their minds, students review their questions and answers. They try to review without looking at the text or, if they wrote notes for Step 4, what they have written. If they did not write notes as part of Step 4, they do so now.

How Else Can We Use This Strategy?

Question Sort: Students generate questions before reading and sort their questions into categories. They answer their questions after reading and then follow through with reciting and reviewing.

Where Can We Learn More?

Anderson, T. H., & Armbruster, B. B. (1984). Studying. In P. D. Pearson, R. Barr, M. L. Kamil, & P. Mosenthal (Eds.), *Handbook of reading research.* New York: Longman.

Robinson, F. P. (1970). *Effective study* (4th ed.). New York: Harper & Row.

Tompkins, G. E. (2004). *Fifty literacy strategies: Step by step* (2nd ed.). Upper Saddle River, NJ: Prentice Hall.

48

Stop-and-React

Suggested Grade Levels: 3 to 8

Elements Addressed: Plot/theme, expository text

Meta-Strategies Incorporated: Making inferences (predicting), summarizing and synthesizing

Supplies: Text that includes a lot of suspense and surprise and provides opportunity for students to predict what's next, lined paper, pens or pencils

WHAT IS STOP-AND-REACT? ●

Stop-and-react is a strategy that forces students to think about what is happening while they are reading.

When Do We Use It?

Students stop-and-react to a piece of literature throughout the process of reading it.

Why Do We Use It?

Stop-and-react increases students' awareness of the text as they read.

How Do We Use the Stop-and-React Strategy?

The teacher prereads the text and determines appropriate places for students to stop reading and react to what they have read. If students are to read independently, the teacher announces stopping points and has the students write down those places before they begin reading. If the reading is to be aloud, the teacher will simply announce when it is time to stop.

Students begin reading or listening as the text is read aloud. At the predetermined points, reading stops and students write their responses to the text so far. They may comment on something that surprised them, express questions they have about the text, or predict what will happen next. After everyone has written something, students share their responses and explain why they responded as they did. The class may chart their responses as a group, with categories of "Surprise," "Questions," and "Predictions," for example.

Students read the next section and again stop and respond. This time, their responses may include comments about the accuracy of their former predictions. Discussion follows, and the process continues.

How Else Can We Use This Strategy?

Stop-and-Draw: Instead of writing responses, students create illustrations in reaction to the reading. This variation works well for younger children or for struggling readers.

Independent Work: Students respond in journals without following up with class discussion.

Where Can We Learn More?

Oczkus, L. (2004). *Super six comprehension strategies: Thirty-five lessons and more for reading success.* Norwood, MA: Christopher-Gordon.

Tompkins, G. E. (2004). *Fifty literacy strategies: Step by step (2nd ed.).* Upper Saddle River, NJ: Prentice Hall.

Figure 48.1

Stop-and-React

Based on the Novel *Stone Fox*

> **Stop reading for a moment on page 78. Reread these lines:**
>
> **"Is she dead, Mr. Stone Fox? Is she dead?"**

On the guide below, describe what is happening in the story. Think about how the characters feel at this moment. Think about how you feel at this moment reading the story.

Description of the Event:

_____

_____

_____

_____

Describe How the Characters Feel:

_____

_____

_____

_____

Little Willy:

_____

_____

Stone Fox:

_____

_____

Describe How YOU Feel:

_____

_____

_____

_____

_____

Book used: Gardiner, J. (1980). *Stone Fox.* New York: Harper Trophy, HarperCollins.

Figure 48.2

Stop-and-Draw

Title of Book: _____

Author: _____

Stop and draw three times during your reading.

1. Read to page ___. Stop and draw a picture of something important that has happened.

2. Read to page ___. Stop and draw again.

3. Read to page ___. Stop and draw again.

Contributed by Julie Song, San Francisco, CA, Summer 2004.

49

Storyboard

Suggested Grade Levels: K to 8

Elements Addressed: Plot/theme

Meta-Strategies Incorporated: Summarizing and synthesizing

Supplies: Any story; board or flipchart and dark-colored marker; drawing paper; crayons, colored pencils, or markers

WHAT IS A STORYBOARD? ●

A storyboard is a graphic, chronological depiction of the major events in a piece of literature.

When Do We Use It?

Students create a storyboard after they have finished reading a piece of literature.

Why Do We Use It?

The storyboard forces students to recall plot incidents and arrange them in sequence. It allows students to use their creativity to depict a story.

How Do We Use Storyboards?

After students finish reading a story, they discuss it as a group. Together, they recall six or eight major events of the story, and the teacher records them on the board or on a piece of chart paper. The group may put the events in correct sequential order, or the teacher may leave that task to individuals.

Students divide a piece of drawing paper into six or eight sections—enough to accommodate all major events. They then illustrate the major events in sequence. Written explanations or quotations from the book may be added.

How Else Can We Use This Strategy?

Independent Work: Older students determine major events independently, without class discussion.

Where Can We Learn More?

Johnson, T. D., & Louis, D. R. (1989). *Bringing it all together: A program for literacy.* Portsmouth, NH: Heinemann.

Schulz, A. R. (1998). *Supporting intermediate and secondary readers: Selected interactive approaches.* Costa Mesa, CA: California Reading Association.

Tompkins, G. E. (1998). *Language arts: Content and teaching strategies* (4th ed.). Upper Saddle River, NJ: Prentice Hall.

Figure 49.1

Book used: Krensky, S. (1998). *How Santa got his job.* New York: Simon & Schuster.

Contributed by Brooke Nylen, San Francisco, CA, Fall 2003.

Figure 49.2 Story Board Template

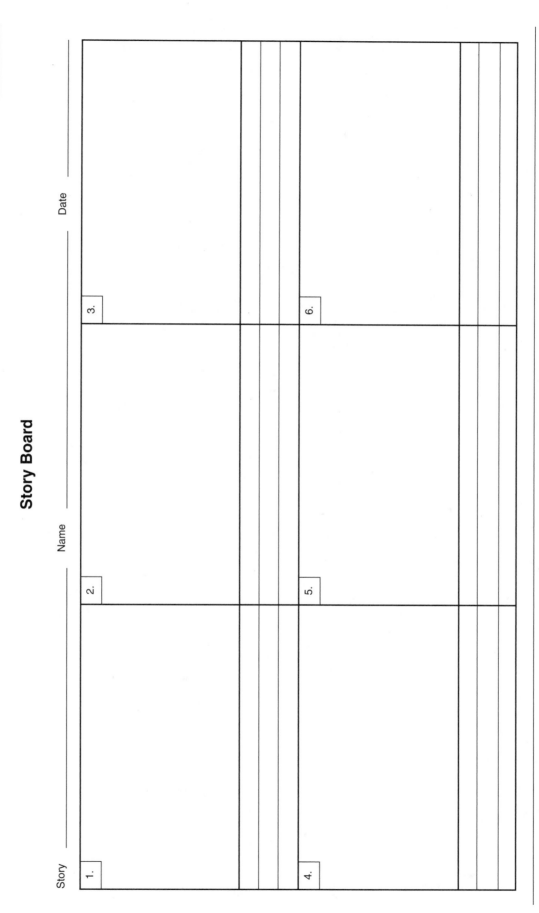

Story Board

Story _____ Name _____ Date _____

1.

2.

3.

4.

5.

6.

Copyright © 2006 by Corwin Press. All rights reserved. Reprinted from *60 Strategies for Improving Reading Comprehension in Grades K – 8*, by Kathleen Feeney Jonson. Thousand Oaks, CA: Corwin Press, www.corwinpress.com. Reproduction authorized only for the local school site that has purchased this book.

Story Frame

> Suggested Grade Levels: K to 5 (and less able readers in the upper grades)
>
> Elements Addressed: Plot/theme, character
>
> Meta-Strategies Incorporated: Monitoring reading for meaning (clarifying), summarizing and synthesizing
>
> Supplies: Any text with a story line, story frame worksheet, pens or pencils

WHAT IS A STORY FRAME?

A story frame is an outline on which students write notes about the various elements of a story.

When Do We Use It?

Story frames are best completed after students have finished reading.

Why Do We Use It?

Completing a story frame helps students understand the structure of a story. The strategy requires students to focus on the main characters, the setting, the major events, and the conclusion of a story.

How Do We Use Story Frames?

Before students begin reading, the teacher leads a discussion about various elements of a story: setting, characters, conflict, solution, and ending. The teacher shows a story frame outline written on chart paper, the board, or an overhead transparency. The story frame outline has on it the following aspects of the story:

- Setting
- Characters

- Problem or conflict
- Solution
- Ending

After students finish reading, they look at the first line or set of key-words on the frame and then offer responses. Frames are relatively open-ended, and no specific words or answers are intended for each blank. The teacher moves the discussion to subsequent lines of the frame. The students are asked to think back to the first line and add information from the story that will make the different lines in the frame relate to one another.

After students have learned to use story frames in a group situation with the teacher's coaching, they begin to use them individually. The teacher reproduces the story frame outline on paper. After students finish reading, the group identifies the different elements and discusses them. Students then have time to work independently to fill in their story frames.

How Else Can We Use This Strategy?

Variations: The teacher can create story frames designed to highlight specific aspects of the literature being discussed. The outline may be made more simple or more complex by reducing or increasing the number of main events included from the story.

Where Can We Learn More?

Coverdell World Wise Schools. *Reading and responding.* Retrieved on June 28, 2004, from http://www.peacecorps.gov/wws/educators/index.html

Cudd, E. T., & Roberts, L. L. (1987). Using story frames to develop reading comprehension in a first grade classroom. *The Reading Teacher, 41*(1), 74–81.

Fowler, G. L. (1982). Developing comprehension skills in primary students through the use of story frames. *The Reading Teacher, 36*(2), 176–179.

Johnson, T. D., & Louis, D. R. (1987). *Literacy through literature.* Portsmouth, NH: Heinemann.

Figure 50.1

Story Frame

Title: _____

This story takes place _____.

_____ is an important character

in the story who _____

_____

_____ is another important character in the story who

_____. A problem occurs when

_____

_____. After that, _____

_____ and _____

_____. The problem is solved when _____

_____. The story ends when _____

_____

Copyright © 2006 by Corwin Press. All rights reserved. Reprinted from *60 Strategies for Improving Reading Comprehension in Grades K – 8*, by Kathleen Feeney Jonson. Thousand Oaks, CA: Corwin Press, www.corwinpress. com. Reproduction authorized only for the local school site that has purchased this book.

...ory Mapping

Suggested Grade Levels: K to 8

Elements Addressed: Plot/theme, character

Meta-Strategies Incorporated: Monitoring reading for meaning (clarifying), summarizing and synthesizing

Supplies: Any text with a story line, story map worksheet or drawing paper, pens or pencils

● WHAT IS STORY MAPPING?

Story maps are graphic organizers that help students analyze a story. They are used to record characters, plot, and setting (both time and place).

When Do We Use It?

Students complete story maps after they have finished reading.

Why Do We Use It?

When students complete a story map, they learn to identify the elements, theme, and moral of a story. They review the parts of the story and information about the book they have read.

How Do We Use Story Mapping?

This strategy is most successful if the teacher first works through one or more samples with the group as a whole. After students understand the process, they create their story maps in small groups or as individuals.

The teacher provides a story map template for students to fill out. The form of the template may vary, depending on the goals of the teacher and whether the focus is to be on characters, problem and solution, events, or something else.

Often students are asked to recount the events of the story in a story map, first summarizing the beginning, then the middle, then the end.

Students may instead use the map to organize their ideas and list the title, setting, characters, problem, solution, and moral or theme of the story. One simple form has a circle in the center for the title of the story and four lines extending to the four corners of the paper. The lines are labeled "Who (Characters)," "Did What (Plot)," "Where (Setting)," and "When (Time)."

How Else Can We Use This Strategy?

Chronological Story Map: One effective use of the story map is to list a complex chain of events within the story in chronological order.

Story Star: In this type of story map, students draw a large star and write the title of the book in the center. One key point—who, when, where, what, or why—is then entered in each point of the star.

Where Can We Learn More?

Beck, I., & McKeown, M. G. (1981). Developing questions that promote comprehension: The story map. *Language Arts, 58,* 913–918.

Bromley, K. D. (1991). *Webbing with literature: Creating story maps with children's books.* Needham Heights, MA: Allyn & Bacon.

Davis, Z. T. (1994). Effects of prereading story mapping on elementary readers' comprehension. *Journal of Educational Research, 87,* 353–360.

Ekhaml, L. (1998). Graphic organizers: Outlets for your thoughts. *School Library Media Activities Monthly, 14,* 29–33.

Reutzel, D. R. (1985). Story maps improve comprehension. *The Reading Teacher, 38*(4), 400–411.

Smith, C. B. (1990). Story map: Setting, plot, mood, theme. *The Reading Teacher, 44,* 178–179.

Tierney, R. J., & Readence, J. E. (2000). *Reading strategies and practices: A compendium* (5th ed.). Needham Heights, MA: Pearson/Allyn & Bacon.

Figure 51.1   Story Map Template

Story Map

Story Title _____   Name _____

| **The Setting** (Time & Place): |
| **Characters:** |

The Problem

The Goal

Event 1

Event 2

Event 3

Event 4

Event 5

Event 6

Event 7

The Resolution

Copyright © 2006 by Corwin Press. All rights reserved. Reprinted from *60 Strategies for Improving Reading Comprehension in Grades K – 8*, by Kathleen Feeney Jonson. Thousand Oaks, CA: Corwin Press, www.corwinpress. com. Reproduction authorized only for the local school site that has purchased this book.

Figure 51.2   Story Map Template

Story Map for *Rosa's Garage Sale*

Story Title <u>Rosa's Garage Sale</u>   Name _____

The Setting (Time & Place): *Olden days, where the donkey lives, and at Rosa's house.*

Characters: Rosa, Donkey, Rosa's father (Sam, old man), old woman, Debbie, a girl.

The Problem *Rosa doesn't have the money to get the donkey.*

The Goal Rosa wants to get some $$ so she can get the donkey.

Event 1 Rosa sits by the donkey and thinks about how she can make money to have him.

Event 2 Rosa puts things out to have a garage sale, but no one comes.

Event 3 Rosa's father said people can't see the things, so she makes a sign but no one comes.

Event 4 Next, Rosa put her coat up high so people will see the things.

Event 5 People stop, but no one buys anything.

Event 6 A man wanted Rosa's things, but he had no money.

Event 7 Rosa and Sam trade the donkey for her things.

The Resolution Rosa got the donkey.

52

Story Prediction Guide

> Suggested Grade Levels: 3 to 8
>
> Elements Addressed: Plot/theme
>
> Meta-Strategies Incorporated: Making inferences (predicting)
>
> Supplies: Narrative or expository text, drawing paper, pens or pencils

● WHAT IS A STORY PREDICTION GUIDE?

A story prediction guide is a booklet make from a piece of paper folded into quarters for recording predictions.

When Do We Use It?

This strategy is best used between chapters of a novel.

Why Do We Use It?

The story prediction guide helps students analyze their reading and ask questions in order to predict what might happen next.

How Do We Use Story Prediction Guides?

Use of this strategy is most effective if the class works through one prediction guide together before students work independently.

When students are ready to begin, the teacher instructs them to fold a piece of paper into quarters, folding first lengthwise and then crosswise. Students are told that they will need to stop reading at specific times to predict what will happen next. The teacher announces four different page numbers (and paragraph numbers, if necessary) for the students to write down so they will know when to stop reading—one stopping point for each page.

The teacher then explains the process. At the designated pages and paragraphs, students stop reading and predict what will happen next, taking the time to think carefully before making a guess. Then they write down their prediction, one on each page of their guide, and explain their reason for their guess. Students are warned that their prediction may not always be correct, but it should be reasonable and fit with the story. They may use their own experiences as part of their explanation.

Students continue through the reading assignment, stopping at each of the designated places to make their prediction. At the conclusion to this activity, students revisit the story and reflect on their predictions.

How Else Can We Use This Strategy?

Predicting Outcomes: Instead of determining stopping points in advance, the teacher has the students read until a certain time and then stop. At a signal from the teacher, students stop wherever they are in their reading, close their book, and use all of the information they have to predict events in later chapters.

Story Prediction Chart: Students receive a story prediction chart or draw their own on paper. The chart has three columns. On the left are listed chapters. In the middle is a column labeled, "What I predict will happen." On the right is a column labeled, "What actually happened." Before beginning each chapter, students predict what will happen and explain briefly why they think that. Then they fold the chart lengthwise so they cannot see their prediction. After reading, they fill in the column about what actually happened. Then they unfold the chart and compare the columns.

Where Can We Learn More?

Daines, D. (1982). *Reading in context areas: Strategies for teachers.* Glenview, IL: Scott, Foresman.

Garrison, J. W., & Hoskisson, K. (1989). Confirmation bias in predictive reading. *The Reading Teacher, 42* (March), 482–486.

Landenwich, M. F. (2001). *Matching reading models and strategies.* NWP Interactive. Retrieved from http://www.writingproject.org/pub/nwpr/quarterly/2001n04/landenwich.html

Morrow, L. M. (1984). Reading stories to young children: Effects of story structure and traditional questioning strategies on comprehension. *Journal of Reading Behavior, 16,* 273–288.

Nichols, J. (1983). Using prediction to increase content area interest and understanding. *Journal of Reading, 26.*

Richek, M. A. (1987). DTRA: Five variations that facilitate independence in reading narratives. *Journal of Reading, 30.*

Figure 52.1 Template for Story Prediction Guide

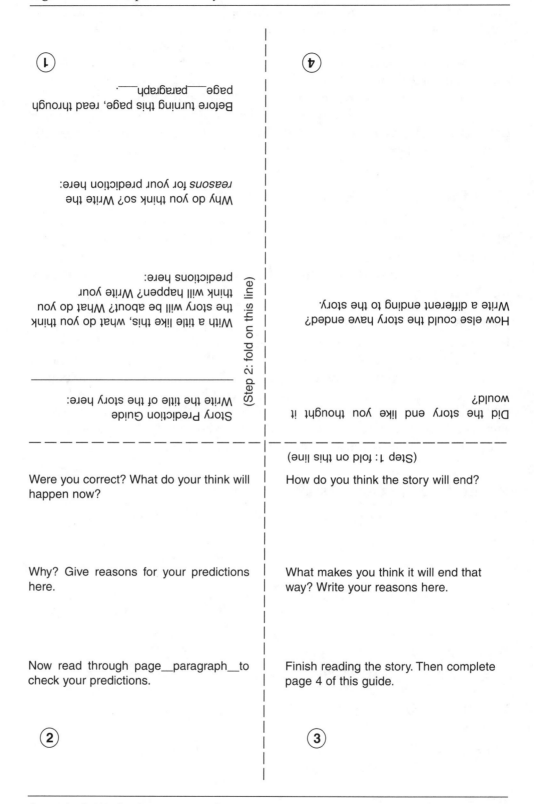

Were you correct? What do your think will happen now?

Why? Give reasons for your predictions here.

Now read through page__paragraph__to check your predictions.

②

③

How do you think the story will end?

What makes you think it will end that way? Write your reasons here.

Finish reading the story. Then complete page 4 of this guide.

Copyright © 2006 by Corwin Press. All rights reserved. Reprinted from *60 Strategies for Improving Reading Comprehension in Grades K – 8,* by Kathleen Feeney Jonson. Thousand Oaks, CA: Corwin Press, www.corwinpress. com. Reproduction authorized only for the local school site that has purchased this book.

Figure 52.2

Story Prediction Chart

Instructions: Fold chart between the "What I predict" and "What happened" columns. Complete "What I predict" before reading. Then turn the chart over, read, and fill out "What happened" without looking at your previous prediction. Finally, compare the two columns.

	What I predict will happen	**What actually happened**
Chapter 1		
Chapter 2		
Chapter 3		
Chapter 4		
Chapter 5		
Chapter 6		

53

Story Pyramid

Suggested Grade Levels: 3 to 8

Elements Addressed: Plot/theme

Meta-Strategies Incorporated: Determining important information, summarizing and synthesizing

Supplies: Narrative or expository text, lined paper, pens or pencils

● WHAT IS A STORY PYRAMID?

A story pyramid is a structured format students use to summarize the most important parts of a story.

When Do We Use It?

Students create a story pyramid after they complete their reading.

Why Do We Use It?

This strategy forces students to review and summarize the main points of a story.

How Do We Use Story Pyramids?

After reading, students summarize the main aspects of a story in a pyramid form with eight lines. The teacher may write instructions on the board, provide a handout with instructions on it, or read instructions line by line, leaving time for students to write before hearing instructions for the next line. Students write based on the following guidelines:

Line 1: Name of main character

Line 2: Two words describing the main character

Line 3: Three words describing the setting

Line 4: Four words stating the problem

Line 5: Five words describing one event

Line 6: Six words describing a second event

Line 7: Seven words describing a third event

Line 8: Eight words stating the solution to the problem

How Else Can We Use This Strategy?

Pyramid Form: The teacher may choose to preprint pages with the correct number and placement of blank lines for students to fill in and with instructions for each line on the page. For younger students, the teacher can provide fewer blank lines to be completed.

Where Can We Learn More?

McLaughlin, M., & Allen, M. B. (2002). *Guided comprehension: A teaching model for grades 3–8.* Newark, DE: International Reading Association.

Staal, L. A. (2001). Writing models: Strategies for writing composition in inclusive settings. *Reading and Writing Quarterly: Overcoming Learning Difficulties, 17*(3), 243–248.

Figure 53.1   Story Pyramid Template

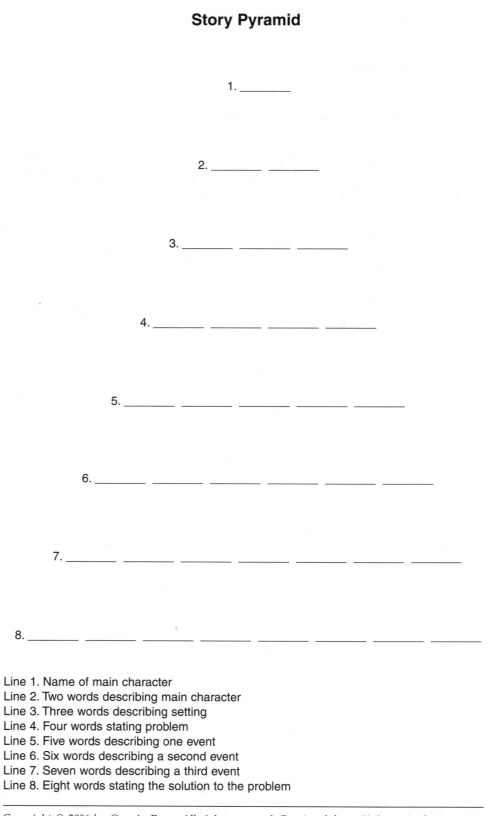

Story Pyramid

1. _____

2. _____ _____

3. _____ _____ _____

4. _____ _____ _____ _____

5. _____ _____ _____ _____ _____

6. _____ _____ _____ _____ _____ _____

7. _____ _____ _____ _____ _____ _____ _____

8. _____ _____ _____ _____ _____ _____ _____ _____

Line 1. Name of main character
Line 2. Two words describing main character
Line 3. Three words describing setting
Line 4. Four words stating problem
Line 5. Five words describing one event
Line 6. Six words describing a second event
Line 7. Seven words describing a third event
Line 8. Eight words stating the solution to the problem

Copyright © 2006 by Corwin Press. All rights reserved. Reprinted from *60 Strategies for Improving Reading Comprehension in Grades K – 8*, by Kathleen Feeney Jonson. Thousand Oaks, CA: Corwin Press, www.corwinpress. com. Reproduction authorized only for the local school site that has purchased this book.

Figure 53.2

Story Pyramid

Line 1: Name of main character.
Line 2: Two words describing main character.
Line 3: Three words describing setting.
Line 4: Four words stating problem.
Line 5: Five words describing one event.
Line 6: Six words describing a second event.
Line 7: Seven words describing a third event.
Line 8: Eight words stating the solution to the problem.

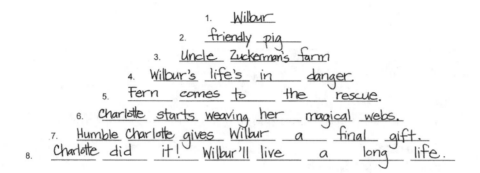

1.   Wilbur
2.   friendly pig
3.   Uncle Zuckerman's farm
4.   Wilbur's life's in danger.
5.   Fern comes to the rescue.
6.   Charlotte starts weaving her magical webs.
7.   Humble Charlotte gives Wilbur a final gift.
8.   Charlotte did it! Wilbur'll live a long life.

Contributed by China Byon, San Francisco, CA, Fall 2003.

Figure 53.3

Contributed by Jennifer Green, San Francisco, CA, Summer 2004.

54

Summary Hand

Also Called: Give Me Five

Suggested Grade Levels: K to 5

Elements Addressed: Plot/theme, character, expository text

Meta-Strategies Incorporated: Determining important information, summarizing and synthesizing

Supplies: Narrative or expository text, whiteboard or flipchart and markers, summary hand forms or paper for tracing own hand, pens or pencils

● WHAT IS A SUMMARY HAND?

Summary hand is a reading comprehension strategy used to help students process key events from stories or summarize *finger facts* from a nonfiction unit. Students organize events or facts on a hand, placing nuggets of information in the fingers and illustrations in the palm of the hand.

When Do We Use It?

Students create a summary hand after they complete their reading of a story or a nonfiction unit.

Why Do We Use It?

With this strategy, students summarize what they have read in an organized form. Using the hand outline, they synthesize new information and information they already have. The form also helps students to review and remember important points, or finger facts, from their reading.

How Do We Use Summary Hands?

After reading a story or an expository text, the teacher begins this strategy by asking students what they know about summarizing. A discussion follows. Next, the teacher draws a large outline of a hand on the board and creates a summary hand, modeling the process and describing it throughout.

For a nonfiction text, the teacher writes the most important facts from the text in the fingers. An illustration goes on the palm of the hand; it may depict one main point or may be a collage of pictures representing all of the facts.

For fiction, the teacher writes one story element (setting, characters, problem, resolution or key event, and ending) in each finger and in the thumb. Again, one main point may be illustrated in the palm, or small illustrations representing several main ideas may be drawn. Alternatively, the illustration may depict a lesson learned from the reading.

After the teacher has modeled the strategy, the class works together to create a summary hand. The teacher reads a story or section from a nonfiction text and asks students to think about the important points. Students share their ideas, and the teacher lists them on the board. Next, students decide as a group which are the most important points, to be included on the hand, and circle them. The teacher or a volunteer writes the points on a clean summary hand.

The next time this strategy is used, the teacher reads to the class or has students read to themselves and then breaks the class into small groups or pairs. Each group or pair receives a summary hand form or is instructed to trace one hand on a piece of paper. Then the small groups complete their summary hands.

How Else Can We Use This Strategy?

Paragraph Writing: Older students may use a summary hand to prepare for writing. The teacher holds up a hand to show how the thumb and pinkie connect. Students write a topic sentence in the thumb, supporting details in the middle fingers, and a concluding sentence in the pinkie. Students then write paragraphs, beginning with their topic sentence from the thumb and following it with supporting sentences from the fingers. They learn that the final sentence (on the pinkie) touches back to the original topic sentence (on the thumb).

Cross-Age Tutors: This strategy works well for older and younger students paired as buddies. The buddies complete the hand together, with each student contributing to the illustration in the palm of the hand.

GIST (generating interactions between schemata and text): This strategy helps students get the *gist* of their reading and works especially well with informational text or with long, difficult nonfiction selections. Student work in groups to discuss meaning, reread text, and reach consensus about statements that summarize the gist of each passage.

Where Can We Learn More?

Cunningham, J. (1882). Generating interactions between schemata and text (GIST). In J. A. Niles & L. A. Harris (Eds.), *New inquiries in reading research and instruction* (pp.42–47). Washington, DC: National Reading Conference.

Oczkus, L. (2004). *Super six comprehension strategies: Thirty-five lessons and more for reading success.* Norwood, MA: Christopher-Gordon.

Figure 54.1

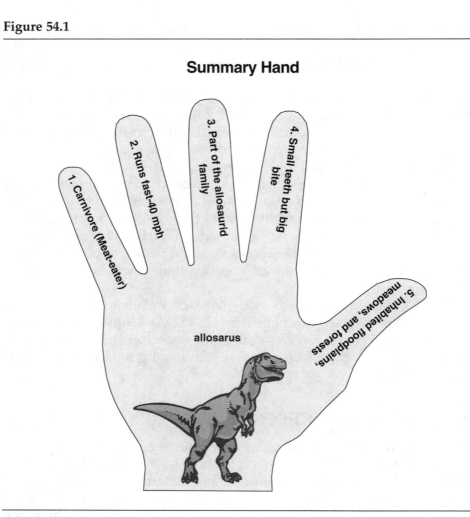

Contributed by Stephanie Chin, Matt Sullivan, and Paola Caoile, San Francisco, CA, Summer 2004.

55

Tableau

> Suggested Grade Levels: 3 to 8
>
> Elements Addressed: Character
>
> Meta-Strategies Incorporated: Making connections, visualizing, making inferences
>
> Supplies: Any text with strong characters

WHAT IS TABLEAU?   ●

Tableau is a physical portrayal of a single scene from a text. Students put themselves in a still-life scene to demonstrate understanding of the text. One at a time, they add movement to their portrayal. This is a variation of traditional role-playing.

When Do We Use It?

Students use tableau during or after reading.

Why Do We Use It?

Tableau taps into the creativity of students who do not work well with words or illustrations; it also benefits students who enjoy the performing arts. Students must visualize and interpret the text to understand and portray a scene; they must also explore characters' behaviors to understand the character.

How Do We Use Tableau?

Students are separated into small groups, and each group chooses a leader. Then, as a group, students select a scene to portray. Each student (except for the leader) represents one character. Students then have time to study that character, learning as much as possible about the character from the literature. (The leader reviews the entire scene, thinking about how the characters interact.) Students portraying individual characters might think about the following:

- How does the character fit into the story?
- How does the character think? Talk?
- How does the character deal with conflicts?
- How does the character relate to other characters?

After students have become experts on their characters, they begin their portrayals, using facial expressions and body language to illustrate the character's traits and characteristics. All freeze with their expressions. Next, the group leader taps one character in the frozen scene, bringing that character to life. Only one character is animated at a time; the characters do not interact. The living character may act and speak as would be appropriate for the scene. Then the leader has that character freeze again and taps another character.

How Else Can We Use This Strategy?

Assigned Scenes: Instead of letting students choose scenes, the teacher assigns them.

Where Can We Learn More?

Wilhelm, J. D. (2002). *Action strategies for deepening comprehension: Role plays, text-structure tableaux, talking statues and other enactment techniques that engage students with text.* New York: Scholastic.

Wilson, G. P. (2003). Supporting young children's thinking through tableau. *Language Arts, 80*(5), 375–383.

Tableau　193

56

Tea Party

Also Called: Literary Get-Acquainted Party

Suggested Grade Levels: 3 to 8

Elements Addressed: Plot/theme, expository text

Meta-Strategies Incorporated: Making connections, determining important information, visualizing, making inferences

Supplies: Controversial text or some other text that invites different perspectives, one index card per student

● WHAT IS A TEA PARTY?

A tea party is a social gathering at which everyone tries to talk with as many people as possible. For a literary tea party, each student receives an excerpt from the text and is told to share that excerpt with as many classmates as possible within some allotted amount of time—maybe twenty minutes.

When Do We Use It?

A tea party works well before reading begins (to help students activate background knowledge and practice prediction skills) or after reading is done (to invite sharing of different perspectives).

Why Do We Use It?

Through this activity, students gain different perspectives on sections of text. Tea parties allow students to think, move about, and interact simultaneously.

How Do We Use the Tea Party Strategy?

Before beginning this activity, the teacher copies one excerpt of text for each student and pastes the excerpts on individual note cards; the cards may then be laminated. Either before or after reading the text, each student draws one card and reads the selection several times. Students first think about the meaning of the excerpt and then practice reading aloud to attain fluency.

Next, the teacher leads a discussion about tea parties, explaining that people at a tea party want to talk to everyone in the room. Students are told to roam the room and find a partner with whom to discuss their quotation; they may discuss *only* the quotations at this party. When they find someone to meet with, one partner reads a quote, and the two students discuss it. Then the other partner reads a quote, and the students discuss that one. Afterward, the partners separate and roam the room to find someone else to share with.

After about twenty minutes, the teacher instructs all students to take their seats. The teacher invites volunteers to share their quotes with the class and tell what they learned from someone they met at the tea party.

How Else Can We Use This Strategy?

Predictions or Impressions: Students read their quotations to partners at the tea party but separate to find new partners without discussing the text. Then, after sharing quotations with as many people as possible, all take their seats. If the activity precedes reading, students in a large group share their predictions about what will happen. If the activity follows reading, students share their impressions.

Question and Answer: Instead of handing out text excerpts, the teacher asks a single question about the reading and then signals students to begin the party. Students discuss their answers to the question in pairs with as many other students as possible.

Where Can We Learn More?

Emery, D. (1996). Helping readers comprehend stories from the characters' perspectives. *The Reading Teacher, 49,* 534–541.

Rowe, D. W. (1998). The literate potentials of book-related dramatic play. *Reading Research Quarterly, 33,* 10–35.

Tompkins, G. E. (2004). *Fifty literacy strategies: Step by step* (2nd ed.). Upper Saddle River, NJ: Prentice Hall.

Wilhelm, J. D., Baker, T. N., & Dube. J. (2001). *Strategic reading: Guiding students to lifelong literacy.* Portsmouth, NH: Boynton/Cook.

Figure 56.1

Tea Party Quotations

From the Novel *The Year of Miss Agnes*

"For another thing, the desks weren't all lined up. Miss Agnes had put them in a circle, around the edges of the room. And her desk was just back in the corner, not where it used to be, in front of the blackboard. "Desks in a circle looked like more fun someway. And a teacher's desk in the corner looked more friendly like, too. Everything was different, but *good* different."	"We had a whole bunch of teachers since they started the school here, back when I was six. Some left before the school year was over. Some stayed one whole school year. But none ever came back after the summer. "Sometimes we could see the look on their faces the first week they were here, cleaning out their little cabin, putting up pictures on the walls. The ones who looked mean from the very first lasted the longest. It was the ones who smiled all the time and pretended to like everything who didn't last."
"There were lots of things we could learn at home, but I liked the stuff we learned at school, too, and I wanted to get good at reading so I could read fast like Old Man Andreson. When the paper comes in the mail from Fairbanks, he reads out loud in the store to everyone, and he goes so fast everyone tells him to slow down. I'd like to read that fast."	"Miss Agnes didn't think school was just for kids. "'You have to keep learning all your life,' she said. "That was a good thing to think about, always learning something new. It wasn't like to you had to hurry up and learn everything right away before the learning time was over, it was like you could kind of relax and take your time and enjoy it."
"With Miss Agnes the world got bigger and then it got smaller. We used to think we were something, but then she told us all the things that were bigger than us, the universe and all that, and then all the things that were smaller. Too small to even see. So people were sort of in between, not big or small, just in between. That was really interesting to think about."	"Writing stories was what I was good at. Miss Agnes said everyone was good at something, and when we asked her to tell us what we were good at, that's what she told me."

Book used: Hill, K. (2000). *The year of Miss Agnes*. New York: Aladdin Paperbacks, Simon & Schuster.

Contributed by Caryn Barry, Jenn Jurcy, and Tobi Slavet, San Francisco, CA, Summer 2004.

57

Think–Aloud Protocol

Suggested Grade Levels: 3 to 5

Elements Addressed: Plot/theme

Meta-Strategies Incorporated: Making connections, monitoring reading for meaning (clarifying), determining important information, asking questions, making inferences (predicting), summarizing and synthesizing

Supplies: Narrative or expository text

WHAT IS THINK-ALOUD PROTOCOL? ●

Using the "think-aloud" protocol, students share their ideas and extend each other's thoughts.

When Do We Use It?

This strategy is used during the reading of any piece of literature.

Why Do We Use It?

Students gain comprehension of a piece of literature as they work in pairs. They freely discuss the literature and help each other interpret what they have read. They also see how others process the material they are reading.

How Do We Use Think-Aloud Protocol?

Working in pairs, students read aloud a section of text and freely express their thoughts about the content. They may point out any problems or dilemmas they encounter, talk about how those problems are resolved, make connections to real-life characters or situations, interpret the section they have read, ask questions, express concerns, or make judgments about what they are reading. Partners respond to each other, helping each other to extend any thoughts.

How Else Can We Use This Strategy?

Teacher "Think-Alouds": The teacher models the strategy (often several times) before asking the students to try it. The teacher reads a line or two from a selection, then stops to think out loud, predicting what might happen next, identifying the problem, making comparisons, commenting on the text, and so forth. In modeling the "Think Aloud" protocol, the teacher shows how good readers automatically ask questions as they read. Teacher "Think-Alouds" help students learn how to make predictions about the text; compare and contrast events, ideas, and characters; visualize the information that is described in the text; and make connections to prior knowledge. After modeling several passages for the students, the teacher can have the students work with partners to "think-aloud" several additional passages.

Where Can We Learn More?

Baumann, J. F., Jones, L. A., & Seifert-Kessell, N. (1993). Using think alouds to enhance children's comprehension monitoring abilities. *The Reading Teacher, 47,* 184–193.

Cullum, L. (1998). *Encouraging the reluctant reader: Using a think-aloud protocol to discover strategies for reading success.* East Lansing, MI: National Center for Research on Teacher Learning. (ERIC Document Reproduction Service No. ED. 420837).

Oster, L. (2001). Using the think-aloud for reading instruction. *The Reading Teacher, 55,* 64–69.

Wilhelm, J. (2001). *Improving comprehension with think-aloud strategies.* New York: Scholastic.

Figure 57.1

THINK-ALOUD PROTOCOL

Based on *Annabelle Swift, Kindergartener*

A pair of students read aloud to one another. Their dialogue sounds like this:

Book: Lucy taped the name tag onto her little sister's blouse.

"Annabelle Swift, Kindergartner!" she read. "I remember my first day of kindergarten, Annabelle," Lucy said importantly. "I didn't have a big sister to train me."

Student A: I remember my first day of Kindergarten, I was so scared!

Student B: I thought I would get lost. What do you think Lucy means by having a big sister to train her?

Student A: I think she means that she didn't have anyone to show her what to do.

Book: Next they went to their mother's dressing table. Lucy coated her lips with lipstick.

Student A: What is a dressing table?

Student B: A table where you get dressed? Look at the picture, it looks like a place where a grown-up would put on make-up or something.

Book: Mr. Blum took Annabelle's hand. "Come join your classmates on the green rug. I'm just calling roll. Watch the other children and you'll know what to do."

Student B: The rug in my kindergarten classroom was blue. And it was a circle, not a square. I used to hate sitting on the rug; I was always squished.

Book: Annabelle sat down. "Drat that Lucy," she whispered to herself.

Student A: Annabelle is mad because nothing her sister told her to do is working.

Book: "My name's Annabelle," she repeated. "Annabelle Swift, Kindergartener!"

Student B: Oh look! Her sister was right after all! She did know things the other kindergarteners didn't know!

Book used: Schwartz, Amy (1988). *Annabelle Swift, kindergartner*. New York: Orchard Books.

Contributed by Kate Working, San Francisco, CA, Fall 2003.

58

Think-of-Three

> Suggested Grade Levels: K to 8
>
> Elements Addressed: Plot/theme, expository text
>
> Meta-Strategies Incorporated: Determining important information
>
> Supplies: Narrative or expository text, think-of-three forms, pads of sticky notes, pens or pencils

● WHAT IS THINK-OF-THREE?

Think-of-three is a strategy in which students select three important ideas from their reading or three important facts from expository text.

When Do We Use It?

The strategy is used during reading.

Why Do We Use It?

Think-of-three forces students to listen carefully or to search actively as they read and to think about the main ideas and concepts in a text. Because they are not allowed to write in the books, they mark important passages with sticky notes.

How Do We Use the Think-of-Three Strategy?

Students are instructed to listen carefully and to read along quietly to themselves as the teacher reads aloud from a narrative or expository text. They are to think about which three ideas or facts from the reading are most important. Next, students are told that they will hear or read the text a second time. This time, they are to raise a finger each time they hear what they think is an important fact and to place a sticky note on the text next to the fact. They must stop after they have raised three fingers and posted three notes.

Next, students write their three main ideas or facts on sticky notes. They then attach the notes to a form. Students share the ideas and facts they chose with another student or with the entire class and explain why they chose what they chose.

How Else Can We Use This Strategy?

Rate and Rank the Reading: Students rate and rank the ideas and facts selected from the text according to level of importance.

Get the Facts: Students scan the text, writing down as many facts as they can within a limited time.

VIP (Very Important Places): Students cut sticky notes into pieces so that each piece has some stickiness on the bottom of it. As students read, they place sticky note pieces next to the most important ideas in the text. Teachers tell students how many VIPs to mark, thus limiting readers to important points and forcing them to identify only essential content. After reading and marking passages, students share and compare VIPs with a partner (Hoyt, 2002).

Where Can We Learn More?

Harvey, S., & Goudvis, A. (2000). Determining Importance in Text: The Non-Fiction Connection. In S. Harvey, A. Goudvis, & P. Stratton (Eds.), *Strategies that work: Teaching comprehension to enhance understanding* (pp. 117–142, 282–286). Portland, ME: Stenhouse.

Hoyt, L. (2002). *Make it real: Strategies for success with informational texts.* Portsmouth, NH: Heinemann.

Oczkus, L. (2004). *Super six comprehension strategies: Thirty-five lessons and more for reading success.* Norwood, MA: Christopher-Gordon.

Figure 58.1

Name: _____ Date: _____

Think-of-Three

Directions:

1. Read the text. As you read, think about the important ideas or facts.

2. Revisit the text. Choose what you think are the most important ideas or facts. Mark them in your book with yellow sticky notes.

3. Decide on your *three* most important ideas or facts. Write each one on a sticky note. Place the notes on the spaces below.

4. Share your three important ideas or facts with two other students in class.

Contributed by Julie Song, San Francisco, CA, Summer 2004.

59

Venn Diagram

Suggested Grade Levels: K to 8

Elements Addressed: Plot/theme, character, expository text

Meta-Strategies Incorporated: Determining important information, summarizing and synthesizing

Supplies: Narrative or expository text, whiteboard or flipchart and dark-colored marker; drawing paper, pencils or colored pencils

WHAT IS A VENN DIAGRAM? ●

A Venn diagram is a graphic organizer consisting of two overlapping circles. Students use the diagram to compare and contrast two entities: characters, elements of the plot, settings, experiences.

When Do We Use It?

The Venn diagram is generally used after reading as a tool for comparing and contrasting particular elements of a story. It is sometimes used before reading to organize background knowledge or during reading to organize ideals.

Why Do We Use It?

When students create Venn diagrams, they visually clarify and identify similarities and differences.

How Do We Use Venn Diagrams?

The teacher first leads the class in creating a Venn diagram as a group. For this demonstration, large, overlapping circles are drawn on the board or on a large sheet of chart paper. When students work individually, they draw the two overlapping circles on a piece of paper. In either case, each circle is labeled with the name of one of the things to be compared and contrasted. For example, each circle may be labeled with the name of a character, a setting, or an event.

Next, students think about traits, characteristics, or facts representing the two entities. Anything characteristic of only one entity is placed in the outer area of the appropriate circle. Anything characteristic of both entities is placed in the overlapping section of the circles. Finally, students discuss their work and the contrasts and comparisons they have charted.

How Else Can We Use This Strategy?

Predrawn Form: For younger children, teachers may provide blank Venn diagrams with the circles already drawn. Students fill in the details.

Multiple Comparisons: To create a more complex Venn diagram, older students may draw three or more circles that overlap in the center.

Cross-Book Comparisons: Instead of comparing two elements within a book, students compare elements from two different books. For example, they may compare the main characters from two books.

Self-Comparison: Students compare themselves to a character in the book—or they compare their hometown to the setting in the book.

Where Can We Learn More?

Ekhaml, L. (1998). Graphic organizers: Outlets for your thoughts. *School Library Media Activities Monthly, 14,* 29–33.

Fisher, A. (2001). Implementing graphic organizer notebooks: The art and science of teaching content. *The Reading Teacher, 55,* 116–120.

Hamner, D. (2005). *Introducing the Venn diagram in the kindergarten classroom.* Retrieved March 3, 2005, from http://www.readwritethink.org/lessons

Herrell, A., & Jordan, M. (2002). *Fifty active learning strategies for improving reading comprehension.* Upper Saddle River, NJ: Merrill Prentice Hall.

Merkley, D., & Jeffries, D. (2001). Guidelines for implementing a graphic organizer. *The Reading Teacher, 54,* 350–357.

Tarquin, P., & Walker, S. (1997). *Creating success in the classroom! Visual organizers and how to use them.* Portsmouth, NH: Teacher Ideas Press/Libraries Unlimited.

Tompkins, G. E. (2004). *Fifty literacy strategies: Step by step* (2nd ed.). Upper Saddle River, NJ: Pearson-Prentice Hall.

Yopp, R. H., & Yopp, H. K. (2001). *Literature-based reading activities* (3rd ed.). Boston: Allyn & Bacon.

Figure 59.1

Venn Diagram Suggestions

1. Compare and contrast two characters from the same story or from two different stories.

2. Compare and contrast yourself with a character.

3. Compare and contrast two settings from the same story or from two different stories.

4. Compare two versions of the same story (Three Little Pigs, Cinderella).

5. Compare and contrast two stories from a series (Cam Jansen mysteries, Henry and Mudge stories).

6. Compare and contrast a similar event in two different stories (a birthday party, a holiday celebration).

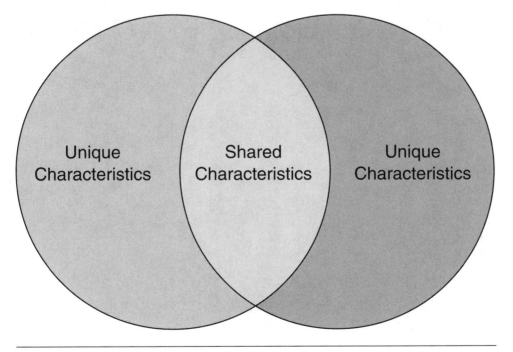

Contributed by Christine Labagh, San Francisco, CA, Summer 2004.

Figure 59.2

Venn Diagram

Based on the books *Wemberly Worried* and *Lilly's Purple Plastic Purse*

Comparison of two characters from two different books by the same author, Kevin Henkes.

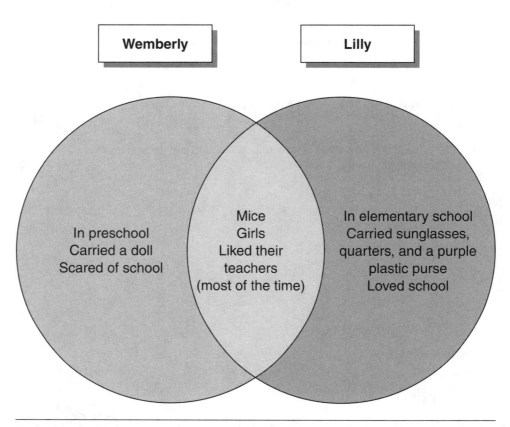

Books Used: Henkes, K. (2000). *Wemberly Worried*. New York: Greenwillow Books, HarperCollins. Henkes, K. (1996). *Lilly's Purple Plastic Purse*. New York: Greenwillow Books, HarperCollins.

Contributed by Kate Working, San Francisco, CA, Fall 2003.

Figure 59.3

Venn Diagram

Abigail Archer's Family

Narrator's Family

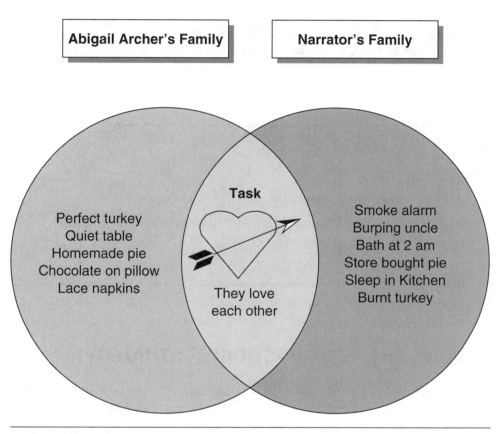

Perfect turkey
Quiet table
Homemade pie
Chocolate on pillow
Lace napkins

Task

They love
each other

Smoke alarm
Burping uncle
Bath at 2 am
Store bought pie
Sleep in Kitchen
Burnt turkey

Book used: Spinelli, E. (2003). *The Perfect Thanksgiving*. New York: Henry Holt.

Contributed by Brooke Nylen, San Francisco, CA, Fall 2003.

60

Yellow Stickies

Also Called: Mark the Spot

Suggested Grade Levels: 3 to 8

Elements Addressed: Plot/theme, character, expository text

Meta-Strategies Incorporated: Determining important information

Supplies: Narrative or expository text, one pad of blank sticky notes for each student, pens or pencils

● WHAT IS THE YELLOW-STICKIES STRATEGY?

Yellow Stickies is a variation of the traditional strategy of highlighting important text or making notes in the margins of a text. Use of the yellow-stickies strategy preserves the condition of the published material, however.

When Do We Use It?

Students use yellow stickies (sticky notes) to record ideas and notes throughout the reading process.

Why Do We Use It?

Many students never learn the traditional and effective strategy of taking notes and highlighting directly in text because they are instructed not to make any marks in borrowed materials. The yellow-stickies strategy allows them to "highlight"—to ask questions, make notes, and respond to the text—quickly and easily without damaging the publication.

How Do We Use the Yellow-Stickies Strategy?

Each student begins with a pad of sticky notes. Using a large book for students in the younger grades or a book with copies for all students in the upper grades, the teacher demonstrates the use of sticky notes to mark places in the text that could be revisited or discussed. The teacher discusses types of things to be marked, depending on the goals of the reading assignment. Students might watch for material related to the following questions, for example:

- Who are the major characters (or personalities in nonfiction)?
- Why did certain events occur?
- What persuasive arguments does the author present?
- What metaphors do you see?

Students are given examples of notes (highlighting facts), responses (personal comments about text), and questions. Then the teacher reads a paragraph and asks students what they might write on a sticky note for the paragraph.

After completing a selection of reading and marking it as a class, students are instructed to follow through independently with more reading. Class discussion follows, with time to answer specific questions.

How Else Can We Use This Strategy?

Color Coding: Students have sticky notes of different colors to be used for different purposes. For example, they might use yellow to address issues of character and green to address issues of theme. Alternatively, they might use yellow for notes, pink for responses, and blue for questions.

Class Symbols: Before explaining the sticky note process, the teacher invites students to develop class symbols to represent thoughts, questions, connections, confusion, and ideas. These symbols are displayed on a large chart at the front of the room. Because students help to create the symbols, they take ownership in the process. They then continue with the sticky note strategy, marking each note with the appropriate symbol, such as a question mark, smiley face, star, check mark, heart, and so forth.

F-Q-R: The process is used to record facts (F), questions (Q), and responses (R). Each note is labeled with one of the letters.

Where Can We Learn More?

Cunningham, P. M. & R. L. Allington (1999). *Classrooms that work: They can all read and write* (2nd ed.). New York: Addison Wesley Longman.

Harvey, S., & Goudvis, A. (2000). Determining importance in text: The non-fiction connection. In S. Harvey, A. Goudvis, & P. Stratton (Eds.), *Strategies that work: Teaching comprehension to enhance understanding* (pp. 117–142, 282–286). Portland, ME: Stenhouse.

Keene, E. O., & Zimmerman, S. (1997). The essence of text: Determining importance. In E. O. Keene (Ed.), *Mosaic of thought: Teaching comprehension in a reader's workshop* (pp. 73–96). Portsmouth, NH: Heinemann.

Oczus, L. (2004). *Super six comprehension strategies: Thirty-five lessons and more for reading success.* Norwood, MA: Christopher-Gordon.

Resource I

Resource I   Strategies Recommended by Grade Level

Strategy	K–2	3–5	6–8
ABC Book	x	x	x
Anticipation Guide		x	x
Bio Poem		x	x
Book Box		x	x
Brainstorming	x	x	x
Bumper Stickers		x	x
Central Story Problem	x	x	
Character Bag		x	x
Character Mapping		x	x
Creating Chapter Titles		x	x
Crossword Puzzle			x
Cubing		x	x
Directed Reading Thinking Activity	x	x	
Double-Entry Journal		x	x
Exclusion Brainstorming		x	x
Fishbowl			x
Found Poem		x	x
Four-Corners Debate			x
Gallery Walk	x	x	x
Grand Conversation	x	x	x
Guided Imagery	x	x	x
Hot Seat	x	x	x
Interior Monologue			x
Jigsaw		x	x
K-W-L Chart	x	x	x
Learning Logs	x	x	x
Life Experience	x	x	x
Literacy Quilt	x	x	x
Literary Sociogram			x

(Continued)

Resource I (Continued)

Strategy	K–2	3–5	6–8
Literature Circles		x	x
Mind Mapping	x	x	x
Open Mind Character Analysis		x	x
Paired Retellings	x	x	x
Pick-a-Pal	x		
Plot Profile		x	x
P-M-I Evaluation (Pluses–Minuses–Interesting Aspects)		x	x
Quaker Reading		x	x
Question–Answer Relationships	x	x	x
Questioning the Author		x	x
Quickwriting	x	x	x
Readers' Theater		x	
Read-Pair-Share		x	x
Reciprocal Questioning (ReQuest)		x	x
Response Log		x	x
Semantic Mapping	x	x	x
Sketch-to-Stretch	x	x	
SQ3R (Survey-Question-Read-Recite-Review)			x
Stop-and-React		x	x
Storyboard	x	x	x
Story Frame	x	x	
Story Mapping	x	x	x
Story Prediction Guide		x	x
Story Pyramid		x	x
Summary Hand	x	x	
Tableau		x	x
Tea Party		x	x
Think-Aloud Protocol		x	
Think-of-Three	x	x	x
Venn Diagram	x	x	x
Yellow Stickies		x	x

Resource II

Resource II Elements Addressed Through Strategies

Strategy	Plot/Theme	Character	Expository Text
ABC Book	x		x
Anticipation Guide	x		x
Bio Poem		x	
Book Box	x		
Brainstorming	x	x	x
Bumper Stickers	x	x	x
Central Story Problem	x		
Character Bag		x	
Character Mapping		x	
Creating Chapter Titles	x	x	x
Crossword Puzzle	x	x	x
Cubing	x		x
Directed Reading Thinking Activity	x	x	x
Double-Entry Journal	x	x	x
Exclusion Brainstorming	x	x	x
Fishbowl	x	x	x
Found Poem	x	x	x
Four-Corners Debate	x		x
Gallery Walk	x	x	x
Grand Conversation	x	x	x
Guided Imagery	x	x	
Hot Seat		x	
Interior Monologue		x	
Jigsaw	x		x
K-W-L Chart		x	x
Learning Logs	x	x	x
Life Experience	x	x	x
Literacy Quilt	x	x	

(Continued)

Resource II (Continued)

Strategy	Plot/ Theme	Character	Expository Text
Literary Sociogram		x	
Literature Circles	x	x	
Mind Mapping	x	x	x
Open Mind Character Analysis		x	
Paired Retellings	x	x	x
Pick-a-Pal		x	
Plot Profile	x		
P-M-I Evaluation (Pluses–Minuses–Interesting Aspects)	x		x
Quaker Reading	x	x	x
Question–Answer Relationships	x	x	x
Questioning the Author	x		x
Quickwriting	x	x	x
Readers' Theater	x	x	
Read-Pair-Share	x	x	x
Reciprocal Questioning (ReQuest)	x		x
Response Log	x	x	
Semantic Mapping	x		x
Sketch-to-Stretch	x	x	
SQ3R (Survey-Question-Read-Recite-Review)			x
Stop-and-React	x		x
Storyboard	x		
Story Frame	x	x	
Story Mapping	x	x	
Story Prediction Guide	x		
Story Pyramid	x		
Summary Hand	x	x	x
Tableau		x	
Tea Party	x		x
Think-Aloud Protocol	x		
Think-of-Three	x		x
Venn Diagram	x	x	x
Yellow Stickies	x	x	x

Resource III

Resource III   Strategies Used Before/During/After Reading

Strategy	Before	During	After
ABC Book			x
Anticipation Guide	x		x
Bio Poem			x
Book Box	x		x
Brainstorming	x	x	x
Bumper Stickers		x	x
Central Story Problem	x		x
Character Bag		x	x
Character Mapping			x
Creating Chapter Titles		x	
Crossword Puzzle			x
Cubing			x
Directed Reading Thinking Activity	x	x	x
Double-Entry Journal		x	x
Exclusion Brainstorming	x	x	
Fishbowl			x
Found Poem		x	x
Four-Corners Debate		x	
Gallery Walk			x
Grand Conversation		x	x
Guided Imagery		x	x
Hot Seat		x	x
Interior Monologue		x	x
Jigsaw		x	x
K-W-L Chart	x		x
Learning Logs		x	x
Life Experience	x		x
Literacy Quilt			x
Literary Sociogram		x	

(Continued)

Resource III (Continued)

Strategy	Before	During	After
Literature Circles	x	x	x
Mind Mapping		x	x
Open Mind Character Analysis		x	x
Paired Retellings		x	x
Pick-a-Pal			x
Plot Profile		x	x
P-M-I Evaluation (Pluses–Minuses–Interesting Aspects)	x		x
Quaker Reading		x	x
Question–Answer Relationships			x
Questioning the Author		x	
Quickwriting	x	x	x
Readers' Theater			x
Read-Pair-Share		x	
Reciprocal Questioning (ReQuest)		x	
Response Log		x	
Semantic Mapping	x		x
Sketch-to-Stretch		x	x
SQ3R (Survey-Question-Read-Recite-Review)	x	x	x
Stop-and-React		x	
Storyboard		x	x
Story Frame			x
Story Mapping			x
Story Prediction Guide		x	
Story Pyramid			x
Summary Hand			x
Tableau		x	x
Tea Party	x		x
Think-Aloud Protocol		x	
Think-of-Three		x	
Venn Diagram	x	x	x
Yellow Stickies		x	x

Resource IV

Resource IV Meta-Strategies Addressed

STRATEGY	Making Connections	Clarifying	Determining Importance	Visualizing	Asking Questions	Making Inferences	Summarizing
ABC Book			x				x
Anticipation Guide	x				x		
Bio Poem	x					x	x
Book Box	x					x	
Brainstorming			x				x
Bumper Stickers						x	x
Central Story Problem		x	x			x	x
Character Bag							x
Character Mapping				x		x	x
Creating Chapter Titles			x				x
Crossword Puzzle		x			x		x
Cubing							x
Directed Reading Thinking Activity		x				x	
Double-Entry Journal	x						
Exclusion Brainstorming					x	x	
Fishbowl	x				x		
Found Poem		x	x				
Four-Corners Debate							x
Gallery Walk	x				x		x
Grand Conversation	x						x
Guided Imagery				x			
Hot Seat					x	x	x
Interior Monologue						x	x
Jigsaw			x		x		x
K-W-L Chart					x		x

(Continued)

Resource IV (Continued)

STRATEGY	Making Connections	Clarifying	Determining Importance	Visualizing	Asking Questions	Making Inferences	Summarizing
Learning Logs		x	x				x
Life Experience	x			x			
Literacy Quilt			x				x
Literary Sociogram		x					
Literature Circles	x	x	x	x	x	x	x
Mind Mapping		x	x				
Open Mind Character Analysis		x	x				
Paired Retellings			x				x
Pick-a-Pal	x						x
Plot Profile			x				x
P-M-I Evaluation (Pluses–Minuses–Interesting Aspects)	x		x				x
Quaker Reading	x	x					
Question–Answer Relationships					x	x	
Questioning the Author		x	x		x	x	
Quickwriting	x						x
Readers' Theater	x			x		x	
Read-Pair-Share					x		x
Reciprocal Questioning (ReQuest)		x			x	x	x
Response Log	x						x
Semantic Mapping		x				x	
Sketch-to-Stretch				x			x
SQ3R (Survey-Question-Read-Recite-Review)					x	x	x
Stop-and-React						x	x

STRATEGY	Making Connections	Clarifying	Determining Importance	Visualizing	Asking Questions	Making Inferences	Summarizing
Storyboard							x
Story Frame		x					x
Story Mapping		x					x
Story Prediction Guide						x	
Story Pyramid			x				x
Summary Hand			x				x
Tableau	x			x		x	
Tea Party	x		x	x		x	
Think-Aloud Protocol	x	x	x		x	x	x
Think-of-Three			x				
Venn Diagram			x				x
Yellow Stickies			x				

Index